Ticking Along
with the Swiss

© Dianne Dicks 1988
ISBN 0-948728-18-3

Cover artwork by Cornelia Ziegler, Basel.

The editor, authors and publishers wish to thank PRO
HELVETIA, the Arts Council of Switzerland, and the Swiss
National Tourist Office for their support of this publication.

Distributed in Switzerland by
GS-Verlag Basel,
Petersgraben 29,
CH-4003 Basel.

Published by: The Friendly Press, Waterford, Ireland.
Typeset by: Adapt Computers, Waterford, Ireland.
Printed in Great Britain by: Short Run Press Ltd., Exeter.

Contents

Introduction

and Warning!

This book is not a travel guide, nor is it the result of scientific study. It is not intended to sell you anything from Switzerland nor to convince you to come here. It contains no propaganda for a special cause and represents no religious, social, political or commercial institution. It has not been written to teach you anything. This book is not like that.

After an English teachers' workshop, Roger Bonner and I were sitting in a Basle café, bemoaning our plight of living in a country where so many people speak English, or at least want to learn it, but where there is almost no market for local English writers. Our conversation went something like this:

"I first learned about Switzerland the hard way. A few weeks after I arrived here, I found myself in the Swiss Army..."

"But that's a fascinating story. You should write about it!"

"Who'd want to read it?"

"I would, and I'll bet a lot of others would too. I know so many foreigners living in this country who have such interesting stories to tell. I wish I could convince English-speaking immigrants to Switzerland like you to get your impressions of living with the Swiss down on paper."

"You should meet Stanley Mason. He's a translator too but a terrific writer and poet. He's probably got a whole stack of tales for you. And I'm sure Riz Careem would write something humorous about running a curry restaurant."

"You know what? I'm going to write to them and ask them to send their stories to me. How soon can you get your army story to me. Let's see, who else could we ask?"

"How about Patricia Highsmith?"

There I was rolling up my sleeves, convinced we had hit upon a good idea that was, at least, worth a try.

A letter was sent to a selection of people 'inviting' them to send me their impressions in English about living in Switzerland. No one was asked to cover a specific topic nor to avoid criticism where it was due.

The stories started coming in. My 'invitation' must have been copied and passed all over Switzerland as I started getting calls from people I had never heard of, telling me about the experiences they wanted to write about. They told me about stories I knew I would like to read. Every few days, thick envelopes arrived in my mail. After reading only a few of the stories sent to me, I was convinced this project would be worthwhile. I knew I could not just send them back. I typed them into my computer and kept my sleeves rolled up. A hobby turned into a hankering. You've got the results in your hands.

Some of the best stories are not included here. Writing is hard work and unfortunately, in spite of my trying to encourage the authors and extend deadlines, many stories that were promised never arrived. What a pity! I hope publication of this book will make these people pull out their dusty and smeared notes and give it another try. I intend to continue collecting stories for the next edition of TICKING ALONG WITH THE SWISS. Why?

Millions of people live some place far away from what was once called home. Newspapers, magazines and bookstands are full of stories about refugees and the masses of human beings moving around seeking some humble existence somewhere on this earth. Their stories are dramatic, full of hardship, destitution and pain. Reading about these tragic cases shakes our confidence in mankind. We begin to question what we call 'civilization' and 'progress'. These are stories everyone should learn about but they will never be stories one can enjoy reading. Their struggles are too distant from those most of us have. Maybe future editions of TICKING ALONG WITH THE SWISS will include stories collected from such refugees in English. But, by chance, the stories in this edition are not like that. They are entertaining, sometimes amusing, sometimes dead serious, full of trivialities, varying sincerity, nonsense and pleasure.

When discussing this book project, sometimes I heard comments like "What could possibly be interesting about living with the Swiss?" "What stories could come from a clean and tidy country that has successfully managed to stay out of wars for many years and maintain one of the highest standards of living on earth?" "With the abundance of violence, sex, scandal and adventure around us, who wants to read stories about casual human encounters in a peaceful country?" "Don't the English-speaking immigrants to Switzerland have an easy time compared with the hoards of other foreign laborers?" "Who cares anyway?" Such comments made me realize why it is hard to find what I call a 'good book' anymore. As the stories were coming in, I was encouraged by the fact that everyone who read them was unable to forget them easily.

Some people have asked me, "What variety of English is valid for Switzerland?" Not so long ago it used to be chiefly British and the Swiss considered anyone not using the grammar, usage, pronunciation and intonation of the BBC to be uneducated and uncouth. TV, tourism and computers have had their impact and now the Swiss often pick out the best from several varieties of English and make up a bit of their own. It is becoming difficult for anyone to keep apart the various English varieties used in Switzerland. This landlocked country finds itself situated in the mid-Atlantic as far as English is concerned. Neutrality is still flourishing out there.

If your mother-tongue is English, you may feel challenged to accept the spectrum of expressions found in this work. If you have studied the influences upon English from the sundry nationalities using this language in Switzerland, you are probably qualified to write an article about it for the next edition of TICKING ALONG WITH THE SWISS. Maybe you would have been stricter and tried to make the stories conform to American or British English. But I am a soft-hearted editor. I could easily talk myself into leaving the exotic gardens of words as they were rather than turn them into orderly but dull fields with no weeds. Living in an orderly country has helped me to appreciate the charm of individuality and to cherish the inevitability of imperfections.

If your mother-tongue is not English, you may be disappointed that there is not a glossary explaining some of the difficult English expressions. Is it a good idea to stop a story-teller and discuss the meaning of words? Why stop reading and start digging through dictionaries? Most of the expressions you do not understand may not mean that much anyway and eventually when you see them often enough, you will understand their meaning. Read and relax, guess the meaning of anything you do not understand. If that seems like hard work, go on to another story. People only work hard at reading when they are being paid for it or if they are teachers and they want to prove to you that they understand something you do not. If you want to understand the meaning of something, you will.

Footnotes are included about some expressions used in Switzerland that are difficult to avoid when talking about living here in English. They may be of special interest to readers involved in the social aspects of language contact situations.

If you have ever lived anywhere abroad or are contemplating or dreaming of doing so, keep reading. As asked in one article in this book, how far away from home do you have to go to become a foreigner? It might even happen to you in your own country. When you feel like the world has stopped and let you off, for better or for worse, you go through some interesting experiences. You look around and are suddenly aware of views you had never noticed before. You start climbing new paths. When you start learning a new language, you leave the security of the sounds and expressions familiar to you from 'home'. No matter how peaceful and affluent the new environment is, no matter how gentle the new language you have to learn is and no matter how kind the people around you are, facing a new culture can be a mind-blasting experience. You may never learn what hit you.

All the authors have lived many years in Switzerland and become properly acquainted with this country, its inhabitants and its problems. Each author has in his or her own way overcome the culture and language barriers to become a part of Switzerland. These stories may not show how they did it, only that it can be done. They will not move any mountains but they might stir up some dust in this tidy country and motivate others to evaluate their inter-cultural encounters from some new and enjoyable viewpoints.

It was my intention to encourage English writers living in Switzerland, but it backfired. No one has been encouraged by work on this book as much as I have. I wish to express here my thanks to all the authors for your cooperation, trust and patience. The work on this book has been like the assembly of a precious Swiss watch, piece by piece, tick by tick. It is a special challenge to bring out a book as teachers' resource material for use in adult classrooms around the world where English is being learned as a foreign language.

Roger Bonner has been a tremendous help in the selection, editing and careful evaluation of these stories. I wish also to thank Tony Obrist, Annette Keller, Anne-Louise and Mitchell Bornstein for their very beneficial assistance and suggestions. I am very grateful to my husband, Walti, for his persistent encouragement and to my teenagers, Martin and Loretta, for sustaining cheerfully the many hours I communicated with my computer instead of them.

Riehen, Switzerland.
August 1988.   Dianne Dicks.

Tic-Tac, Tic-Tac

by Stanley Mason

When we lived in Trollbrunn, a lady by the name of Frau Huber lived opposite us. Huber is a common-or-garden name in those parts of Switzerland, and Frau Huber did it justice. She was in no way unusual, in fact she seemed to embody all the endemic qualities of the local populace. She was reserved, order-loving, quiet and respectable. She had lost her husband some three or four years before and she dressed in the dark, nondescript clothes that befit a widow. She was thin and almost a little ascetic in appearance, but with a square and rather determined jaw. She seemed to have no particular friends and was never to be seen gossiping in the street like some of the other women. When she met you she would greet you very politely, and if you chanced to find yourself standing beside her in a queue she would exchange a few remarks about the weather which confirmed exactly what you already knew about it, and she would always add that this sunny dry weather, even if rather hot, was just what we had long been waiting for, or that this wet, cool weather was really very necessary at this time of the year.

Frau Huber swept the drive in front of her house every day, and there could be no doubt that the flat she had on the first floor was equally clean and tidy, though perhaps simple and a little old-fashioned. I can very well imagine what it looked like, even though I never saw it, for she never invited anybody in. She spoke to all the neighbours, of course, and was well regarded by everyone, but she seemed to have no friends and no relations.

We had a very good refuse collecting organization in the parish of Trollbrunn, as in fact everything in those parts was very efficiently organized. The ordinary garbage was collected twice a week and had to be put out on the pavement in sacks before eight o'clock (because the refuse lorry passed at that time) at a point that was marked by three yellow crosses. Then the bulk rubbish collection came every second week and took the things you were not allowed to put into the ordinary garbage, such as ashes or bundles of stalks and twigs from the garden (they had to be cut to a maximum length of one metre). Twice a year there was a service called the landfill collection which took bigger things, such as pieces of old bedsteads. In addition there was a special metal collection from time to time, as well as collections of glass, papers and old clothes. The whole system was, as I have said, very well organized, but it was a little confusing for ordinary mortals, as nobody could keep all the dates in his head on which all these various waste collections took place. Here Frau Huber was a very great help, for she knew it all as though by second nature, and by seven thirty in the morning she had already put out whatever it was they were going to collect that day. You had therefore only to look out of the window after seven thirty (supposing you were up by then) to know what rubbish you could get rid of on this particular occasion.

To this day the world-famous hand-made embroideries of Appenzell are made at home. Photo SNTO.

Frau Huber lived opposite us for several years. She went about her daily round unobtrusively, sweeping her drive, going to shop at the local grocer's with the same grey shopping-bag, politely passing the time of day with all and sundry. Once or perhaps twice she even went away for a few days with a small attaché-case, though nobody knew just where she had gone.

On sunny days she would go out and work in the garden. You couldn't see what she grew in her garden or what she did there, as it was screened from the road by a tall arborvitae hedge. But on the days when they collected garden refuse, you could see the stalks of achillea neatly bundled on the pavement at seven thirty of the morning, or in late autumn those of her fading chrysanthemums.

There were times when I personally felt just a trifle sorry for Frau Huber. What had she to expect of life? She had lost her husband, she seemed to have no relatives or friends. What makes such an existence worthwhile? On the other hand, she went about her daily round like clockwork, she was fit and active despite her being well over sixty and very thin. She never showed any sign of needing consolation, or even any desire to come any closer to people in her neighbourhood, to share any human warmth or compassion they might have to give. She had a square jaw and an upright stance.

One day we got the news that Frau Huber had been taken to hospital. We missed her in the next few days. The leaves began to collect in her drive. And gradually I began to have a bad conscience. Ought I not to go and visit her in hospital? There would surely be hardly a soul who would go and visit her. Wasn't it a neighbour's duty?

So I went and paid her a visit. She was in the general ward, rather pale, looking straight ahead. It was not easy to make conversation with her.

"It's very nice of you to have come to see me," she said. "It's a little boring to lie in bed with nothing to do. But the nurses are very kind."

They were going to operate on her next day, she said. "At nine fifteen," she said, and looked at her watch. It struck me that she would have said "At nine seventeen and a half" in just the same matter-of-fact tone.

I made conversation with her as well as I could.

"If anything should happen to me," she said after a while, "I should like you to have my chrysanthemums. There are twelve big plants just under the kitchen window. I know you appreciate flowers. Just go and get them."

Three days later we got the news that Frau Huber had died after the operation.

The funeral took place on the following Wednesday. There were very few mourners, just a few neighbours. On the following Saturday I went and dug out the chrysanthemums. I didn't really need any chrysanthemums, but I felt it was a matter of piety.

Old Frau Müller was there when I arrived. She was taking a few hortensias from along the hedge, and before I went Herr Haller from up the road came to get the dahlias.

I had almost got over Frau Huber's passing – although I admit it worried me in a strange, subliminal kind of way – when I got a letter from a small local fiduciary company. They invited me to telephone them and arrange a meeting in connection with the estate of Frau Agathe Huber deceased.

Two days later I was ushered into a dark office in the next town where a man with a hearing aid and a large black moustache shook me by the hand. He condoled with me on the loss of Agathe Huber (which made me feel slightly ashamed, perhaps because I had not even known her first name till I had seen it in his letter) and said that she was a rather unusual case, as there were no relatives once or even twice removed and the small sum of money she had left had therefore gone to her husband's brother, who was still alive but an inmate of an old people's home. However, she had left a will and in it had bequeathed to me a gold watch which had apparently belonged to her late husband.

He thereupon handed me a gold wristwatch, a rather antiquated model with a worn leather strap, but obviously a quality product in its day. And of course, gold.

"I've wound it up and checked its time-keeping," he said. "It still goes perfectly, to the minute."

Slightly at a loss, I took the watch, signed the paper he placed before me, shook him by the hand and went. What exactly had I done to deserve even an old-fashioned gold watch? I had never done more for Frau Huber than to bid her good-day and to exchange comments about the weather.

When I got home, I took the watch out of my pocket and looked at it. It was going smoothly, tic-tac, tic-tac. I already had a watch and had no need for it. Nor was there anybody I could give it to. It served no practical purpose. And yet it went on ticking, accurately, reliably. Its hands moved towards no future fulfilment, it had no destiny or destination any more, yet it went on running, tic-tac, tic-tac, obeying the inward law that was built into it from the first. Towards what? I could not help thinking of Frau Huber. She too had gone on ticking, accurately, reliably, when there was nothing left to tick for. I even thought about the rest of us, going about our daily rounds, year in, year out. Towards what? In fifty years we shall all be forgotten. In a hundred or so there will not even be a faint memory of us left in the fading senses of the last aged contemporary. Yet we go on running, tic-tac, tic-tac.

The following week I saw a job in the paper for an engineer in a small town near Rome. I applied at once. I think perhaps it's always a mistake to stay too long in one place.

Winter in the Ticino

by Patricia Highsmith

Winter in the Ticino is indeed different from the Ticino's summer. In summer it is full of tourists in search of sun, and the hotels of Lugano and Ascona are full up during the Locarno Film Festival, causing police to shoo away the blue jean set before they bed down in the public parks. Sleeping outdoors is not allowed, not even in the woods all around.

In winter one can park one's car rather easily in the main part of towns and do some shopping. But Locarno, for instance, is by no means empty, and looks like a normal town, with enough people to form queues at the supermarket, and to make the main department stores look as if they are doing normal business. The customers are the real *Ticinesi,* plus a handful of foreigners who now make the Ticino their home.

It is the year-round dwellers who are apt to complain about the winter dullness. "Nothing's alive. Haven't you noticed that?" Of course I had noticed it. People don't hurry. Lots of restaurants and hotels are closed. I happen to like the quiet.

I live in a village much quieter than Lugano or Locarno, in summer and even in winter. The village in winter has some hundred and five inhabitants. An English friend just spent a few days with me and remarked that the village looked quite without inhabitants. We had walked to the post office and encountered one person besides the postman in his little bureau.

I look out of my windows, upstairs and down, on gray granite roofs of smallish houses, most built about two hundred years ago, as

The outside walls and the roofs of the houses in the valleys of Canton Ticino are made of broken stone. Photo SNTO.

was my house. The windows are rather small. Picture windows would be quite out of place in this peasant architecture, not to mention that building restrictions forbid such innovations when doing up an old house. The village sits on one side (the side with less sun in winter, as it happens) of the Valle Maggia, and has two main streets parallel to each other, paved but one-lane, causing cars to move slowly. There is no bakery or butcher, but a small grocery shop exists for staples. One trattoria serves as bar-café, and provides hot meals if you get there on time to meet their chef's hours. There's wine, of course. Everyone drinks wine here and also grappa. A village man sells his home-made grappa for twenty-five francs per liter, and very good it is, either neat or tossed into a cup of espresso.

Around my horizon, the great silent mountains stand, white-capped since November, not from snow of which we have had none as yet and it's early February, but from height. In September the mountains were all green with pine trees, chestnut and sycamore, and now under their white tops the green has turned to brown and is darkening. The purity of the mountains' snowy peaks against the usually clear blue sky is magnificent, worthy of a camera shot, but that is the trouble: these Alps have been photographed too often and have become mysteriously boring, like Beethoven's Fifth. A man from the desert might well stare in wonder at these mountains, unscarred by man, which keep their snow well into June, as if to proclaim their altitude. But if you see them every day they become a familiar background, and one can begin to resent them for blocking the sunlight.

There is only one American, a retired widow, in the region and she lives in Ascona. I recently met an Englishman. Most of my friends are German-speaking, and are either from Germany or are German-Swiss. There are also a few writers and painters from Germany who have come to the Ticino perhaps because of the cultural attachments begun by the many Germans who settled here at the end of the nineteenth century.

I get together with some of these people every week or so for dinner at someone's house or mine. "Food is important here," a friend remarked to me, "because there's nothing else that's very amusing." So hosts and hostesses try to do their best in their cooking (effort and obvious trouble are highly praised). It is customary to bring a little present when one comes to dinner. This can be a plant in a pot, a cake from a good bakery, and it can also be a pain if you haven't acquired something the last time you went shopping and there is nothing around the house appropriate as a *Mitbringsel***. There are no drinks-before-dinner as the English and Americans know it, but possibly an appertif of wine or maybe sweet vermouth, followed by dinner. People happy on wine can sit up shouting political arguments at one another until two in the morning. More sedate people say good night at ten or before. For one thing, the mountain roads, always winding and often just wide enough for two cars to pass, are very dark in winter after six in the evening, and the driving of the *Ticinesi* is not so disciplined as that of *Baslers* and *Zürchers*. And one drunken driving offense can get one's license removed for six months.

February 6, and the first snowfall during the night. It is hardly two inches deep. A friend rings up from the next valley. "Take a look at the road and ring me back at noon." The surface of the little road below my house looks dark, meaning the snow is melting, so

** *Mitbringsel,* a gift for the host.

my friend will arrive at half past one, after listening to the
*Frühschoppen*** program noon to one on her telephone-radio. Here
everyone has the telephone-radio which works on the telephone
system and has six stations and no static. The mountains make
reception difficult. My portable Grundig does quite well and in the
small hours of the morning picks up the World Service.

Early December is like the dead of winter here. I had the feeling
of living in a submarine. The submarine is my house. It is a two-
storey narrowish house of stone with two cellar levels. The great
weight of granite tiles on the roof is supported by long old rafters of
hard chestnut, but the outer walls are of natural stones of all sizes and
shapes, selected and laid upon one another, without cement. The
walls are a meter thick at least. The lower cellar's two rooms are like
dungeons with arched ceilings lined with round stones the size of
oranges and grapefruit. Four pieces of granite project from the walls
of each dungeon to hold lengths of red chestnut wood, now sagging
with time. These crosspieces were to keep cheese and hams out of
reach of mice and rats. I have never seen a rat or a mouse here, but
once I found a snake in the second cellar. In the dim electric light
there, I thought it was a piece of chrome and picked it up. The snake
was afraid and wriggled off. Probably it had come to shed its skin in
a quiet place. The silence in the second cellar rooms has to be heard
to be believed. It is as if the world had ceased to exist. The only noise
is that of the blood going past my eardrums.

The submarine atmosphere also prevails in the upper two storeys
in winter. I get out of bed at nine or so in the morning, turn on the
light to make coffee in the kitchen, then a second light to read the
newspaper which has arrived at eight-forty-five. The village post
office is open from quarter to eight till quarter past in the morning,
and at two other periods of the day, the three of which one soon
memorizes. The great use of electric light is normal in the Ticino,
even for people who live in newer houses with larger windows than
mine. Switzerland was never famous for sunlight, because of the
mountains. I think this can have a depressing effect, a feeling of being
closed in, with consequent emphasis on self-sufficiency, tendency to
smugness, maybe alcoholism in the types prone to it. This may not
apply to the *Ticinesi*, who keep more to the Italian way of life. I notice
among the outsiders like me who live here, that a great deal of time
is spent in relating real or imaginary slights, insults, neglects,

** *Frühschoppen*, a popular TV and radio program, now discontinued.

attitudes, to any friend or ally who will listen. Maybe it is because the community is small, and little new blood comes in. Or does the Ticino make people nervous?

As for oddballs, within and mostly without my circle, the region abounds. One elderly *Ticinese* woman has a grown-up mongoloid son who comes and goes, and innumerable cats that she feeds on bread and milk only, though the cats look marvelously healthy because they beg from other houses. She lives alone, her alcoholic husband having long since drifted away. She is said to be well-off, but she wears an old housedress and apron, never sweeps the stone floor of her kitchen, judging from my one glimpse of it, sometimes returns my *"Buon' giorno,"* sometimes not, as if she were miles away in thought.

Just up the mountain lives Herr S., a war veteran, alarmingly thin and with a heart condition. Nobody seems to like Herr S. because he does not return people's "Good morning" in any language. But I have always found him friendly and polite. He thinks people don't like him because he is a German. On Christmas Eve just before midnight, I heard a knock at my door. It was not Santa Claus, but to my surprise Herr S. He has no telephone and his electricity had conked out, stopping his oil heating. I rang emergency service in Locarno and spoke in Italian and German to a man who wished me a Merry Christmas. I offered Herr S. coffee and *Stollen*** while we waited. In twenty-five minutes his electricity was back on. Herr S. said the coffee and cake was his Christmas celebration. Indeed, I have never seen a friend come to his house! The next evening, the same thing happened and we had to ring emergency service again. "You don't think they're doing this on purpose to ME, do you?" I said I didn't think so, that there was probably something weak in his electrical system. If the people in a nearby house happen to arrive with their noisy grandchildren, Herr S. will say to me, "They yell on purpose to annoy me!" with a grim, long-suffering look in his eyes.

Recently an energetic German-Swiss broke up a dog fight on the main street with a trattoria chair. He wounded one dog and refused to pay the vet's bill.

A bachelor *Ticinese* neighbour is a vegetarian who believes that massage and herb soups can cure all human ills. Everyone considers him odd. Just after Christmas, I saw that my car parked below had a gray plastic cover on it, with little hooks to keep it in place. I had no

** *Stollen*, a cake.

idea who had put this on, and asked three people if they might have done it, and all said no. Then ten days later, the herb-and-massage bachelor turned up and asked if I liked the car cover. I said I was delighted and hadn't known where it had come from. I was able to give him one of my books in Italian. Compared with his present, I felt mine was not a big one.

For all the quirkiness of people here, the friendliness level is higher than it was for me when I lived in France. The French are like people in an army, though one seldom thinks of the French as soldiers: rather reserved and inhospitable, *chacun-pour-soi* and no-welcome-to-strangers. The Ticino, like Switzerland itself, offers a variety of races and personalities. Everyone here seems to be an individual. Maybe everyone thinks everyone else a bit strange, and from the depths of my submarine in winter, I realise that I may be reaching this point at which I think everyone is a bit cracked except me. What are people saying about me behind my back? Could I face it if I knew?

More snow. At midnight I put on my back-door light. The scene is like an old Christmas card. Big soft flakes drift past the pine trees, past the already white low stone wall that supports the next garden, onto the granite roof of an outhouse across the path going up the mountain. Very silent, and nothing in sight that was made more recently than two centuries ago.

Morning. The snow still falls on horizontal grapevines which were trimmed in October and grow on the granite slabs that form our roofs. Gray smoke rises from a couple of chimneys showing that a few people live here. I work on my electric typewriter under two electric lights. One of my friends is giving a dinner party next Friday. There is another friend in Lugano who may think I am neglectful because I had to decline her last invitation and haven't communicated since. The herb-and-massage man has gone to his Ascona apartment to spend the rest of the winter. The dog-basher is holed up, at work on interior tiles in his house, a do-it-yourself man.

An eighty-two-year-old woman clumps through the snow with a big tapering basket full of kindling slung on her back. My English acquaintance remarked that since this old woman had just sold some of her land for a million Swiss francs, she could afford to hire somebody to haul her firewood. I thought of Elvis Presley, dead at forty-four because he changed his life-style too radically. It is pleasing to see these *Ticinesi* who may have become 'rich', though you could never tell it from looking at them, keeping to their old ways, eating in their kitchens which are part of the living room.

February 8. Snow forty centimeters deep, very fluffy, the kind good for snowballs and snowmen. We have all had snow tires on our cars since November. The Cantonal roads will soon be cleared by machine. The little roads in villages present the difficulties, if any. People will shop less frequently in Locarno and Ascona, bringing home all the food they can. The two cinemas in Locarno are showing mediocre and popular films, all dubbed in Italian. Everyone is working on something, and I am too, and what people say about me out of my hearing doesn't bother me, yet.

The Ticino, like any region of character, cannot be altered to fit. You have to fit yourself in or not. It offers beauty, quiet if one wants it, easy access to Italy, pleasant train service to Zurich, whence one can fly off anywhere. Most people like friendly people, and I am certain that the people here are friendlier than the people 'up north'. The Ticino is also a mysterious place, composed of a lot of granite said to have a magnetic effect, draining one's energy. A friend in Zurich tells me the Ticino makes her tired. Can this be true? I was advised to take walks – to find sunlight and to escape this gravity pull. How can one escape the density of rock, even if one climbs the highest mountain? Usually it is the individual who creates his own mental state and invents his own illnesses. Every few days I push button three on my radio for the express purpose of restoring my sanity with a few minutes of classical music. But doesn't everyone do something like this every few days?

Patricia Highsmith. Photo J. Bauer.

A shortened version of this story was first published in German in MERIAN, July 7, 1983, *"Untergetaucht im Tessiner Winter"*

An A-Z of Life in Switzerland

or

Foibles are Other People's Customs

Compiled by Jeffrey Barnes, Scott MacRae and John Purnell

Sketches by Marsha K. Browne

Apfelstrudel tends to be eaten with cold, or at least tepid, custard. The slimy yellow substance is referred to as *'Vanillesauce'*. It's surprisingly delicious, though - knocks the spots off the Spotted Dick with Custard we got at skool.

Bünzli. According to a Swiss colleague, I'm one for unwrapping my homemade sandwiches in the train instead of patronizing the restaurant car or minibar. Personally, I don't think sweaty cheese between doorstep slices of brown bread can be described as *bünzlig*, which better describes my fellow passengers who prefer to remain hungry till they reach their destination. *Bünzli* could be translated as *petit bourgeois*.

Classes, such as we are used to in Britain, do not exist in Switzerland, and those that do are less obvious because the dialects of Swiss German tend to be regional rather than class- oriented. But on closer observation some subtler distinctions emerge.

One is the carrying of briefcases. The well-worn, mock-leather briefcase, containing perhaps an apple or other *Z'nüni* snack and a copy of the tabloid 'BLICK', is a hallmark of the working man. Every morning, hordes of them can be seen alighting from suburban trains at Pratteln, Schlieren and other such centres of Swiss industry.

Executive types, by contrast, will brandish an attaché case, while youngish people with sympathies for an alternative life-style are now no longer ashamed to cycle to work with a small rucksack on their backs. (Only a few years ago I was laughed at for doing so, as the use of rucksacks was then limited strictly to hikers and gnarled mountain-dwellers.)

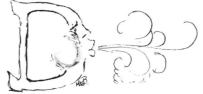

Draughts. When you travel in packed trains during the heat of summer in northern Switzerland, your opening a window will draw hand-gestures and irate cries of *"Es zieht!**"* from your fellow passengers. This problem does not seem to exist in the French-speaking part of Switzerland. There, with Gallic vigour, the locals throw the train windows open wide and enjoy the sort of air conditioning that used to capsize large sailing boats. Speaking for myself, I find these gusting Force 8's a good thing on a warm day. I dare say this difference in national character might produce friction if ever the two temperaments should meet. Fortunately, the SBB have anticipated the problem by introducing air-conditioned carriages with windows that won't open. The problem doesn't exist on the Jungfraubahn either, but this is not a good example because you're hard pressed to find any Swiss on a Jungfrau train. It does however prove that the Japanese are fond of fresh air.

** *Es zieht,* "There's a draught!"

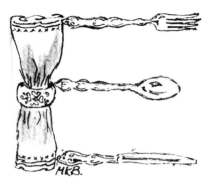

En Guete. Fortunately, few Swiss make any attempt to render this dialect term in English. Corresponding to the standard German *Guten Appetit!* this has to be said to one's table companions before starting a meal and one soon gets used to it. A problem for newcomers to Switzerland is the variety of ways in which *en Guete* is pronounced in the different dialect regions, which means that they can, and do, interpret it as anything from communal throat clearing to an introduction of a discussion on the greatest writer that the Big Canton (Germany) has produced. In fact, lunchtime conversations about Goethe might well be more common in Britain and the United States where, far from wishing others an enjoyable meal, it is often better to come up with something to take their minds off it.

Fires. I recently took some visitors from the UK on a walk in the northern Jura hills. We trekked for a few kilometres through delightful woodland and great tracts of rolling meadow, and then stopped to admire a particularly fine view. At this point, one of my guests asked me why the remains of so many little camp-fires were dotted all over the place. After years of hiking in Switzerland, I am used to this feature of the better known rambling routes. As I explained to my companions, many German-speaking Swiss on a long walk feel they must stop at some point and build a fire. The only things that will prevent them from doing so are heavy rain, lack of wood, inappropriate terrain or forest-fire warnings.

In the preferred walking seasons of spring and autumn, you see countless little groups sitting around fires roasting sausages which have first been given the criss-cross of ritual cuts to prevent them from exploding in the flames. Welcome as these delicious snacks are after two or three hours of strenuous hiking, I am convinced that the main purpose of the exercise is building the fire. There seems to be some deep, atavistic compulsion behind it. Far from trying to analyze it, I now find my own eyes automatically scanning the forest-floor for kindling and choosing a likely little clearing for the sacred flame.

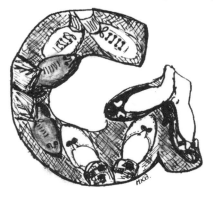

Greeting. When I was dispatched to Switzerland I had some small knowledge of what to do in terms of social conventions. I had been told to shake hands with everyone I met. But nothing had prepared me for the complex rituals involved in greeting people here. This is a very serious affair. Non-observance of these Swiss customs might expose you as an uncouth foreigner and a simple situation might get a little out of hand.

Take for example behaviour in lifts. Members of other nations tend to regard a lift as a functional object, a way of getting from A to B. You just get in, push the button and go your own way. If other people get in, you treat them with studied indifference. Not so in Switzerland! In an office building here the trip is the setting for a minor social gathering. When getting in, you greet the other occupants cordially. They are your fellow passengers for the voyage, your comrades of circumstance. Paradoxically, after these warm exchanges, lift-riders tend to study their feet with such intensity that you find your own eye inexplicably drawn to other people's shoes.

The Swiss penchant for hoping that you do not suffer too horribly from the vicissitudes of the day/afternoon/evening/etc. is a little bewildering if you should feel there are more important things in life than Nice Days, etc. If such greetings were restricted to the vernacular, they could be regarded as a charming national whimsy, but when translated into English, as they frequently are, they come over as faintly ludicrous.

An essential element of greeting in Switzerland is the handshake. You absolutely have to shake hands firmly every time you meet, even if this is underwater, as happened with a Swiss teacher friend who met a pupil of hers in the swimming pool. If the person's right hand is not available (due to injury while doing something recreational in the Alps, for instance), then you may lightly touch his or her right outside elbow or left hand.

Holes. Large groups of people stand around in Swiss cities looking down holes. Unlike the French, who are obsessed with gorges (see the Michelin Guide to France), the Swiss are only fascinated by big man-made holes in which construction work is going on. Although building sites are popular in other countries, it is hard to imagine that the fervour felt among the Swiss spectators could be matched elsewhere. I was once quietly reading a newspaper on a tram when my fellow passengers, almost to a man, suddenly leapt up and flung themselves to the windows on one side, making the vehicle lurch sickeningly. They just wanted to look at the progress being made in one of the city's main holes of the moment.

The country certainly provides devotees with a great deal of material since modern building techniques, sometimes with the additional influence of regulations for nuclear shelters and underground car-parks, make for major excavation sites in all the towns. Some truly magnificent holes have been dug for the construction of the Zurich S-Bahn (urban railway). Outside the cities there are all the tunnels through mountains, of course.

I first became aware of the national importance of holes when the local council decided to build an enormous new sewer passing just in front of my flat. Some of the shafts for the sophisticated tunnelling equipment, about which much was written in the local press, were sunk right outside my window. As the number of spectators grew, observation platforms were put up for them. I realized that the audiences were made up of all classes and age groups, though the most ardent and best represented fans were certainly the pensioners.

A retired neighbour of mine, with whom I had previously had little contact, seemed to feel genuine pity at the fact that I had to work and therefore almost always missed the best of the action. He took to lying in wait for me in the evenings and giving me detailed, even impressively technical (i.e. incomprehensible) progress reports. I initially found these a little irksome but later tended to miss them on the days when he did not turn up. It proved to be only a short step from the building site to coffee and cake with this neighbour and wife. I suppose a lot of friendships come into being around these holes in the ground. But this social function does not entirely explain their pull. Another reason is probably a desire to see taxes being sensibly spent on public-sector building projects. Then there is the Swiss fascination with efficiently working machinery in action and new technology proving its worth. The construction workers too, many of them from southern Europe, often put on a good show, quite consciously playing to their audience.

When the sewer was finished, but mercifully before it became operative, the council actually staged an 'open house' in it with drinks and sandwiches and explanations of methods and equipment. Literally hundreds of people came.

The disadvantage of all this excavating and tunnelling is that Switzerland must now resemble a huge Emmental cheese. No doubt, one day a last, crucial shaft will be sunk and the whole country will fall in on itself.

Invitations to Swiss households are rare. If you get one it's likely to be fixed some weeks or even months in advance. To phone up a Swiss acquaintance and suggest coming over the same day tends to be regarded as a gross invasion of privacy – worse even than telephoning someone after 9 pm. Rudest of all is to drop in unannounced. Such spontaneous visits are dreaded by the Swiss housewife. She won't have had time to tidy up and may not have the necessary tidbits to accompany coffee.

Further detracting from spontaneity is the need to bring a gift. While original *Mitbringsel*** are usually welcome, the following guide of standard offerings may prove useful to the uninitiated:

	Required value:	Acceptable gifts:
Weekend invitation with overnight stay	Sfr. 30-40	Magnum of good-quality wine, bottle of liqueur, or extra-large (two tiered) box of chocolates, and if the hosts have children about half the quota may be spent on sweets for them. Household item also acceptable if known to be useful.
Whole-day, dinner or party	Sfr. 15-25	Good French or unusual Swiss wine, or perhaps even a couple of bottles of Italian or Spanish wine providing it's a *Geheimtip**** (not, of course to be consumed the same evening, but stashed away in the cellar and never mentioned again), standard size of chocolates or bunch of flowers.
Short visit, e.g. for *Z'vieri*	Sfr. 7-20	Cake (may be homemade if of professional quality), small 'token' box of chocolates, small bunch of flowers or perhaps (since flowers are overpriced and short-lived) a potted plant.

Jass is a card game that is, and always will be, a complete mystery to any foreigner living in Switzerland. If you've sussed it out (in which case you'll already have your red passport and your place at the *Stammtisch*****), good luck to you!

** *Mitbringsel*, a gift for the host.
*** *Geheimtip*, an insider's tip.
****Stammitsch, a restaurant or a pub table for customers who meet there regularly.

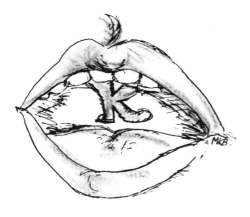

Kehlkopfkrankheit - an affliction of the larynx – is how other nationalities speaking German regard the Swiss dialect because of the harsh fricatives that issue from the back of most Swiss throats whenever a word containing a 'k' or a 'ch' is uttered. English speakers may find it a rather baffling but likable language quite different from German and without its more sinister and arrogant tones. After a few years in Switzerland, one learns not only to understand Swiss German but also to appreciate the incredible variety of dialects that coexist within such a small area. By that time, the German we learned at school will have become lilting and interspersed with Helveticisms, making us an object of amusement or even incomprehension when we go to Germany. As a result, we develop the same feelings of wariness and envy when confronted with an overbearingly fluent German, as many Swiss admit to having.

Late. Swiss guests will cheerfully stay at a party until 4 am on a weekday, but the same people will apologize elaborately for telephoning after 9 pm. Like most of the customs we discuss in this A - Z, the attitude is infectious: "Sorry for calling you at such a late hour. Hope I'm not disturbing you" (at 21.20 hours) as one of my co-authors said to me recently.

Museums. There are excellent museums in Switzerland's cities, but some of the smaller provincial ones, like the museums of Roman antiquities in Augst and Nyon, are real gems. At the most appropriate times for visits, i.e. wet weekend afternoons, you only see people from the English-speaking countries in them. When do the Swiss go?

Newspapers in Switzerland are remarkable for their variety and quality. The Swiss very often don't appreciate it. There are frequent complaints, for instance, about the BASLER ZEITUNG being a 'monopoly'. British cities of equivalent size would be proud to have one paper of its calibre. Even the very substantial TAGES-AN-ZEIGER is compared unfavourably with the NEUE ZÜRCHER ZEITUNG (a truly formidable paper, but who really reads it all?) At the other end of the scale, Switzerland's only real tabloid is as good a contender for the gutter as any of its German or British equivalents. In the middle of the field we have the many small but admirable regional papers whose front pages usually give equal weight to the arms-reduction talks between the Superpowers and the outcome of the last night's local council meeting.

Reading the Letters-to-the-Editor section of any Swiss newspaper is most enjoyable. Here the neutral foreigner can savour the tones of moral outrage targeted on local politicians or journalists for some recent utterance or article. The Swiss themselves are rarely neutral when it comes to the three 'evergreen controversies' – cars (personal freedom versus destruction of the environment), dogs (value to society versus potential health risk) and foreigners (we know this country is too crowded, but Switzerland needs us as much as we need Switzerland).

Newspaper critics in Switzerland are a topic in themselves. Take the film critics of the quality (i.e. most) newspapers, for instance. They sensibly leave it to the reader to decide whether a film is 'good' or 'bad'. But many of them take the lofty view that the plot or (heaven forbid) the 'story' of a film is of secondary importance. What matters to them is the 'subtext'. Therefore they invariably relate every detail of the plot, including the climax of who-dunnits, before claiming that the film, if it is one with a social message, is too *vordergründig***. In other words, they criticize directors for not making the film they (i.e. the critics) think they should have made. They like to see things spelt out. Intimidatingly high-minded though they are, they are as suspicious of a seemingly 'progressive' film (unless from the Third World) as they are of the most reactionary Hollywood Rambo products. Above all, they are hostile to the idea of film as entertainment. Nothing coming out of the USA goes down well with them unless produced before 1947. As friends of Hollywood know, that date marks the end of a period representing the peak of western civilization since the Renaissance. However, Third-World films inevitably meet with their approval. As a rule, the costlier the film, the less they like it. Unless, of course, the director is 'great', in which case they can give full reign to their literary gifts and extend their range of compound nouns. The result is, of course, not so much a review as an essay.

This form is also familiar to Swiss opera critics (who are all men, whereas women are occasionally allowed to write the cinema column). Their review of a first night will be devoted almost entirely to the philosophical, historical, ideological etc. background of the opera. Then they dissect the production. In this respect they are like critics everywhere, but usually being 'progressive', tend to prefer Aida to be a charwoman rather than an Ethiopian princess. They are surely unique, however, in the consistency with which they fail to mention the singers' names. After all, it's only an opera. The whole thing is usually only **sung** from beginning to end. Why bother to mention the singers? A recent example was the review in the Basle newspaper of the 1987 Bayreuth "Lohengrin" in which the leading role was, as other sources readily admitted, very successfully taken by Basle's own much loved and carefully nurtured house tenor. Did

** *vordergründig*, superficial.

the critic in his full-page dissertation on the performance deign even to mention the man's name? No! Nor did the weekly WELTWOCHE, a liberal paper of some quality that seems in any case to take a very jaundiced, or at best patronizing, view of Basle.

Stylistically, Swiss <u>art</u> critics take the cake. Many of them provide, if not an insight into the mind and art of a painter or sculptor, then at least an impressive exercise in German literary comprehension for the reader. "Say not the struggle naught availeth" is what one might murmur while ploughing through, for instance, Sigmar Gassert's stylish reflections in the BASLER ZEITUNG...

Ordnung. The Swiss are no more and no less law-abiding than people of other nations. But they do have, at least in the German-speaking part, a marked sense of what is done, or, perhaps more noticeably, of what is not done. *"Das händ mir nid gärn"* – "We don't care for that sort of thing" – can be the well-meant but often devastating response to one's inadvertent breach of the established order. It may be a breach of the *Hausordnung**.* Like playing a musical instrument at lunch-time, taking a bath after ten in the evening, hanging one's duvet out of a window overlooking the street. It may be something more serious, like washing your car in the street or gardening on Sundays. These activities are claimed by many to be actually illegal, and they seldom go unobserved. Or it may be something less tangible – a breach, say, of the rules of social intercourse and etiquette, like prematurely addressing someone in the familiar *'Du'* form or innocently reverting to *'Sie'*. In the adult world, of course, order is much less concerned with propriety than with convenient, smooth-functioning efficiency. Surely that is the hallmark of Switzerland. *Ordnung muss sein***!*

** *Hausordnung*, the house rules in a flat or apartment building.
***Ordnung muss sein, the battle cry of the *Bünzli*, see first page of this list for the meaning of that.

It sounds hard, doesn't it? But when combined with today's greater tolerance, it is a truism that has lost none of its vitality.

Prejudice. Despite all these generalizations, please don't think we're prejudiced against Switzerland. Such prejudice among foreign observers is all too common and annoying to those of us who have got to know the country properly. Any article about Switzerland in the English-speaking press is bound to contain cynical references to the 'stolid', 'dull' or 'boring' Swiss. (Incidentally, I notice that an engineering firm involved in the construction of the Zurich S-Bahn is called 'Swissboring'.) Cleanliness and order are equated with lack of imagination. The country's wealth is put down to the Mafia money pouring into Swiss bank accounts, the unscrupulous dealings of the Swiss multinationals and Switzerland's 'luck' in staying out of two world wars. There must surely be an element of envy in such criticism. The fact is that in most respects, Switzerland has succeeded where other countries have failed. The Swiss are probably right in believing that this is due largely to hard work and avoidance of confrontation.

Queuing. While being served at the bank or post office, don't be surprised if there is somebody standing right next to you, leaning on your part of the counter and following your business with relaxed and friendly interest. You might also find yourself in a Y-shaped queue. It has a bend in it. Latecomers join it halfway down, thus creating the second arm of the Y. Latecomers may not have noticed the bend, or if they have, they regard the time saved as yet another minor triumph in life's rich fabric...

What about the 'queue' at the butcher's as you cower among the housewifes? Anglo-Saxon inhibition may make you point out that you are not, in fact, next in line. Such distinguished behaviour will probably not win many points at Migros.

Rösti-Border. A gross over-simplification of national eating habits, put about by the Swiss themselves, is that the German-speakers eat *Rösti* and the other linguistic groups do not. Now *Rösti* is a hearty dish. It's made of potatoes that are boiled, grated and fried brown, perhaps with added bits of bacon or other tasty elements. In other words, *Rösti* is rather down-to-earth, not to say peasantish, though unbeatable on a cold, wet evening.

The *Rösti*-border is a sort of Swiss Mason-Dixon line dividing the German-speaking part of the country from the French. Amateur and even professional psychologists may be interested to note that is it known among the German-speakers as the *Rösti*-Ditch and among the French-speakers as the *Rösti*-Wall, terms which conjure up visions of vast defensive structures intended to keep out the barbarians.

Including the *Rösti*-Border in this A-Z is a little unfair, because the subject of the relations between the linguistic groups which make up Switzerland is extremely complex. Any serious consideration of it would imply profound knowledge of national history, geography, economics and constitutional law. Suffice it to say here that there is affection, animosity, co-operation and envy between the groups in question. Somehow they have succeeded admirably in living together with frictions (usually) kept well under control. Even the Swiss themselves find it almost impossible to talk about their *Rösti*-Border without a hint of a smile, and that in itself is a very healthy sign.

Sex. No sex, please, we're British.

Schaffen. You live to work. Work starts at the crack of dawn, or well before it in winter, which involves getting up in the middle of the night. Even if you have flex-itime, it doesn't make a good impression if you traipse in after 8 am. By that time numerous people will have already tried to find you or telephone you. One secretary I knew was at her desk at 7 am every morning from 1945 until she re-tired last year. Conversely, *Feier-abend*** is also to be taken seriously. God help you if you return your dirty cups to the coffee lady just as she is packing up to go home.

Taking work seriously does have its advantages. It's probably the reason we are so well off in Switzerland. It means that you can rely on people. Take, for example, the average Swiss railway *Kondukteur****. He is smartly turned-out, can speak 4 languages, checks your ticket conscientiously, can usually spot the people who have just joined the train, and leaps in and out of the train at each stop. His shambling, ill-dressed British Rail counterpart will scarcely be able to speak English, will often spend the entire journey skulking in the guard's compartment, and, if he had a pint too many the evening before, may not even turn up to work at all, in which case your train will be cancelled. However, if he does get round to checking tickets, you

** *Feierabend*, the end of a working day.
***Kondukteur, the conductor on a train.

probably won't dread his appearance as you do the sound of *"alle Billette bitte!"*** when you've forgotten your season ticket.

Tea in Switzerland can come as a shock to British visitors. Used to a piping hot beverage with the colour (and taste?) of a coalman's armpit, here they are generally confronted with a glass of water that may have been hot when it left the kitchen. Resting on the saucer, or, if you're lucky, suspended in the glass, is an undersized sachet usually proclaiming itself to be 'English Tea' that is barely capable of lending a yellowish hue to the water. This brew (best described by the colloquial British expression 'gnat's pi**') then turns completely white when you add the plastic container of cream provided. If you ask for milk, you will be considered eccentric and will most likely be ignored. The best solution is to give up and order coffee, or perhaps one of the other, healthier forms of 'tea' (e.g. peppermint, scornfully referred to as 'liquid Wrigleys' by a compatriot of mine). If the Swiss order tea, it's usually because they're not feeling well.

Umwelt ('environment', though 'ecology' often fits better) is the Swiss watchword of the eighties. Understandably so. Combating the *Waldsterben* (another watchword that could be translated, albeit inadequately, as 'forest death' or 'decline') may prove to be a question of life or death for many mountain communities and does not merely reflect the 'sentimental feelings towards the forest' that Teutonic peoples are alleged to have. Moreover, Swit-

** *alle Billette bitte*, tickets, please.

zerland's landscape – its greatest, and almost its only natural resource – has been seriously scarred in recent years by new roads and tourist developments. Then came the two environmental catastrophies of 1986: Chernobyl and 'Chernobâle' (the latter being a punning nickname for the fire in a chemicals warehouse near Basle that sent a flotilla of dead fish bigger than the Swiss navy down the Rhine). We have seen energetic campaigning by pressure groups and some surprisingly bold legislation. But the constant exhortations to 'use public transport, save energy, consume less' are unlikely to achieve much in a country where financial incentives are ineffective (everyone in Switzerland can afford to run a car, pay for high energy costs, pitch out their twice-worn clothes and 5-year-old sofas, etc.) and where there is still a vociferous 'personal freedom' lobby. The recent election successes of the *Autopartei*** would probably not have surprised R.A. Langford, who singled out (admittedly in very gentlemanly tones) the aggressive and self-righteous behaviour of Swiss motorists in his book *"England-Schweiz unentschieden"* which was published 30 years ago. At that time, traffic conditions must have been paradisiacal compared with today.

Verboten. In Switzerland most things are forbidden. Everything else is compulsory.

Waschküche (laundry room). The inner sanctum, the Holiest of Holies, where the (not always well disposed) spirit of the house dwells. It is known to all who live

** *Autopartei*, a pro-automobile political party which could be a Swiss backlash against the greens.

in a Swiss flat. It brings out the worst in even the most reasonable and tolerant of tenants. You may successfully avoid any contact at all with your neighbours in the house itself by listening for voices or the rattle of other doorhandles before stepping out into the corridor or by crouching behind your geraniums when your neighbours appear on their balcony. However, encounters (dramatic or otherwise) are inevitable in the laundry room. They may be triggered by anything from having your washing still drying on someone else's washing day, to leaving a red, white and blue sock in the machine (or worse, in the machine's inner works). Has no one ever written a play set in a Basle flat's laundry room? (Entitled, say, "Armageddon".) The *Waschküche* provides a microcosm of life, the stuff of human drama. Sadly, perhaps, all that is required of it is that it be kept clean. Somehow, that hardly seems enough.

Xenophobia is often alleged to be a Swiss characteristic. It is quoted, for instance, as a factor in Switzerland's rejection of UN membership. The non-renewal of the work permits of thousands of foreign workers during the 1970s recession did nothing to improve this reputation. Among ordinary Swiss people there is certainly a feeling that foreigners don't do things properly, and we foreigners sometimes suspect they have a subtle way of talking down to us, namely, by speaking dialect (or our own language) when we speak standard German and by speaking standard German when we attempt valiantly to speak dialect. These days, it seems, the term *Uusländer*** is uttered in a critical tone of voice mainly with regard to refugees from Third-World countries or to the wealthy German owners of holiday homes in Switzerland. The Italian population, by contrast, is now-adays well integrated and we Anglo-Saxons are obviously making a useful contribution to the economy, while the French don't seem desperately keen to live here anyway. Given the size of the foreign community in Switzerland (almost 15% of the

** *Uusländer*, Swiss dialect for 'foreigner'.

population), it is perhaps surprising that there is not more friction. If anything, there would appear to be stronger xenophobic feelings towards the German-speaking Swiss in the French and Italian-speaking parts of Switzerland than towards foreigners (of the right cultural complexion) anywhere in Switzerland.

Yodelling. Much stranger in many ways than Hebridean mouth music or Tibetan belly chanting, yodelling is nevertheless popular throughout much of Switzerland. Far from being restricted to the remoter mountain settlements, thriving yodelling clubs can be found in all Swiss towns. In fact they can be found quite easily if you happen to be within earshot while rehearsals are in progress. There are even yodelling church services, presumably along the lines of 'The Lord be with you-del-di-dee-di-hoo.' Amazingly, the practice seems to have spread all over the world. There are apparently avid exponents in Japan, and it is a fairly frequently used device in Country and Western music.

Yodelling does tend to be like the bagpipes though, you either love it or hate it, and that goes for the Swiss themselves as much as for the rest of us. When done badly, by one of the less talented groups on an off-day for instance, there is no doubt that yodelling sounds incredibly awful – like cats in torment or a bunch of young boars all being castrated simultaneously. Time and place are important factors too. I once literally dived for cover when a large group of yodellers opened up without warning in the grotesquely echoing main hall of one of the country's larger railway stations. On the other hand, few people could help being at least a little moved by a slow, nicely modulated yodelling chant driving over an alpine valley at sunset, like a sort of melancholy vocalized bugle call, punctuated only by the soft resonance of distant cowbells.

Zurich ought really to be the capital of the Republic of *Schweiz*, a German-speaking country in Central Europe. But because the Latins shifted Switzerland's centre of gravity westwards, Berne, the capital of a bilingual canton, was chosen instead. Just as well, perhaps. There can hardly be many towns that radiate so much coldness as Zurich – and it's not just foreigners who think so. During the youth unrest a few years back, rather an effective photomontage was made showing icebergs floating down the Limmat, and one of the organs of the youth rebels was called the *'Eisbrecher**'*. True, Zurich is a beautifully situated and elegant city full of cultural interests and contrasts. On one side of the river, glacial blue trams glide down the opulent Bahnhofstrasse with its exquisite shops and palatial banks while just across the river the parallel Niederdorfstrasse is a bustle of overt whoring and fixing. And yet, like the harsh dialect spoken there, it seems to lack the charm and *Gemütlichkeit**** of Berne and Basle. The uncharitable view is that the latter two cities are tempered by their proximity to national or linguistic borders while Zurich is pure, undiluted, materialistic Switzerland.

Scott MacRae, John Purnell and Jeffrey Barnes. Photo R. Jeck.

** *Eisbrecher*, ice-breaker.
****Gemütlichkeit*, coziness, homeyness.

Living Room

Reflections on close quarters, personal territory and how the Swiss – and I – live with it

by John O'Brien

Scene: People are crowding into a lift in a Swiss company canteen. Just as the door is about to close, someone slips in and chirps, *"Grüezi mitenand!"* (Hello everybody!). "Grüezi," everyone dutifully murmurs. No one seems to know anyone else. Silence. The lift arrives, the door slides open and before emerging, this last-on, first-off passenger trumpets, *"En guete!"* (Have a good appetite!), and unfailingly gets the corresponding reply.

Scene: A crowded waiting room in a dentist's office, anywhere in Switzerland. A newcomer enters and – naturally – mutters the standard Swiss greeting, which is invariably muttered back. And when summoned, the patient never fails to deliver the customary parting shot: *"Adieu!"* It may even be bolstered with the wish that those fellow-sufferers have "A nice day."

Anyone who has lived in Switzerland for any length of time can add dozens of further examples of this seemingly exaggerated politeness, verbosity and effusiveness. What's behind all these good wishes to strangers, this seeming friendliness? Is there really so much brotherly love in this small Helvetic confederation? The answer from this corner is: Not all that much, but brotherly love isn't even the point. These multitudinous polite nothings and seemingly empty phrases have quite another, definite function and perhaps even contain a lesson or two for the rest of us, as I shall attempt to show.

For I have a theory about this quirk of the Swiss. Before going into my theory, however, think upon the word *small*. That's what Switzerland is, and though just about everyone agrees that it's an attractive place to live, there is not much room to do it in. In a country made up of thousands of individual, self-governing communities where residential and industrial areas are rigidly zoned, the land is immutably divided into small plots which are barely sufficient for the population's needs and, inevitably, very very expensive. As a result, there isn't that much room to move around in.

People who live in Swiss cities and towns, particularly, are crowded together morning, noon and night. As someone who has had to come to terms not just with the closeness but with a sense of being crowded, I would like to present the reader with my profound theory, which goes like this.

Any of us can get by without a living room, but none of us can do without living room. It's our inviolate personal territory. Even an animal will jealously defend its territory, as any observer knows. In fact, next to its young or its own life, its territory is one of the very few things an animal will defend even to the death.

We humans each have our personal territories too, and psychologists tell us this is not only our physical dwelling place; we carry our territory around with us, as it were. It can actually be measured in a certain number of inches surrounding our bodies, and it may contract or expand according to whether the person approaching us is an intimate, a complete stranger or someone in between.

Now when an incursion into this 'territory' is threatening or is actually taking place whether by chance or as an unavoidable result of circumstances (as in a crowded lift or tram), we react. But being, as we say, civilized, we don't snarl or bite the intruder; we protect our inviolable territory by ... Well, how do we protect it? How do we handle the situation?

This bit of pompous theory brings me to the Swiss – and to some self-reflection. Looking back on my nigh-on fifteen years of living in Basle, I think that from the very beginning I've never ceased to be struck by the smallness and crowdedness everywhere. People live above you, below you, to the right and left of you and – watch it! – right behind you. Shopping or walking down the street offers rich opportunities for a bit of deft footwork, walking sideways while inhaling deeply. At our neighborhood market, for example, it is impossible for two shopping carts to pass in the aisles; one shopper must back out ignominiously, and, as you can probably guess, it's usually me.

As someone who grew up in the American Midwest and Northwest, I initially treated this facet of Swiss life as a joke; it was rather quaint and fun to back up, nimbly sidestepping fellow shoppers, pedestrians and apartment-house dwellers. But then it began to get on my nerves. I felt crowded, imposed upon and finally, at bay. I wanted to snarl, to shove, to lunge forward with my arms doing the breast stroke and – just to show to what depths I had fallen – not say *"Exgyysi"* and leave out the *"bitte"*!

Yes, I felt that my personal territory, my living room, was being invaded and I had to do something about it. But then I said to myself, "John, old boy, you're going to have to come to terms with this somehow. Why not observe the Swiss themselves and see how they deal with living in one another's pockets?" And then I began to notice: Those eternal greetings and goodbyes and nice days and good appetites and pleases and thankyous and don't-mention-its; they really do make the unavoidable closeness with a total stranger bearable. At any rate, they seemed to make that sensitive no man's land of mine contract, or at least neutralize my feelings of outraged anger. I realized too that you don't feel any longer like shoving or baring your fangs at people who get uncomfortably close when they wish you well for later, after they're out of your way.

One could even get philosophical about the whole thing and ask how, in an increasingly crowded and angry world, are we going to live together? Maybe the Swiss way of handling strangers at close quarters isn't such a bad idea. Not just that it keeps us from going for one another's throats; you might say it shows what makes us different from all other animals – we can talk. More than that, as I ruminated further, it shows we must talk to a complete stranger in certain circumstances, or we will go for his throat, or vice versa. And taking the thought yet one step further, it might not be such a bad idea if not only individuals but groups, races, peoples and countries might try a bit more talking when they're on a collision course – even if it is only making polite noises – before taking hostile action.

Let's see now, where was I? Ah yes; how I, as a native-born American used to wide open spaces, wide roads and wide aisles, came to cramped, crowded little Switzerland and learned to live with it – the Swiss way.

Uh-oh, here comes the old lady who lives on the top floor, making her way up the winding staircase. Looks like I'll have to squeeze against the wall so she won't have to let go of the banister. Here we go.

"Excuse me."

"It's all right."

"Have a nice day."

"Thank you."

"You're welcome".

"Goodbye."

"Goodbye."

You see? I've become an expert.

Sisterhood - does it grow in every climate?

by Heidrun West

I have worked to see myself
through the eyes of my friends,
my neighbors, and my students,
through the eyes of women
I do not even know.
I may have cleared a small stone
here and there
in the path to new relationships,
but it is an uphill job.
Struggling to imagine myself
on the other side of the obstacle
blocking the path -
feeling myself to be 'the other' -
leads to the even greater struggle
of pushing away
this boulder of misunderstanding.
The work seems equally hard
whether it implies reaching out
to a total stranger
or to the partner
who might otherwise become one.

And it takes at least two.

* * * *

I first came to Switzerland with my parents when I was eleven. As refugees from Sudetenland (now Czechoslovakia), we had lived in Germany from 1946 until 1955. Unlike my parents, I was still young enough to learn the Swiss dialect without the accent that would mark me as a foreigner. I was twenty when my British husband and I signed our marriage contract in Geneva in 1965 that read *"l' homme est le chef de la famille et la femme dirige le ménage."* Happy to get married, I had thought this division of roles no more than amusing. A year later my husband and I left for Philadelphia.

When we came back to Switzerland in 1971, we moved to a small farming village at the southern end of the Lake of Zurich. After the dirt, the traffic and the oppressive summer smog over Philadelphia, the clean streets and well-kept houses of this Swiss village were a relief. I had forgotten the joy of petunias, geraniums or carnations decorating windows that were open to the sunshine. And here they were again, the boxes carefully balanced in the white window frames overflowing with blooms bright red, pink, white and blue. They seemed to reach out to me, welcoming me back. The warm air was filled with the clean smell of hay spread out in the sun to dry. Farmers were busy turning it over or raking it into neat rows and piles for the tractors to pick up. The women followed the machines in their wake, raking up the few stalks the tractors had missed. I could not help thinking that this was a good place for our son – barely 18 months old – to start his great adventure of meeting the world.

The five years in America had given me much. I had learned to appreciate the openness with which new ideas were met. I had learned that changes could indeed be brought about, but that their initiation depended on individuals ready to accept the risk changes require. I had also learned that life did not just happen to me, but that I had a choice in directing it. So I started my life in the village, full of energy and good intentions, led by the old proverb 'where there's a will, there's a way.' But I was only twenty-six, too young to understand that my attitude was too different. I was 'American' they said. My offers of help were interpreted as interference; the oatmeal cookies I had passed over the hedge had not left the intended sweet taste. There was much I had to learn.

Our house sits on a plateau about 600 feet above the village, surrounded by 30 or so similar houses. There is a small grocery store a mile from us; the supermarket is in the next little town, two miles from our house. When we first moved here, most of the families had one car. Shopping then was a major expedition. Pushing my son in his stroller, I would walk to the supermarket in the late afternoon. My husband would pick us up there with the car on his way back from work. There were days when our walk past the cows grazing in the fields, past the pretty farm houses with their gardens full of flowers and thriving vegetables was a real pleasure. But there are many days of rain, of fog and ice in this picture-postcard country. And I was pregnant again.

So I suggested to the other women in the neighborhood that we find a way of sharing a car. The general response showed me how little I had grasped the situation. "But then the other women will see what I buy," is what each of them told me. If the words were not identical, the spirit in which they were said was the same.

Most of us had small children, which made it difficult to do anything alone. My trips to the gynecologist were exercises in keeping my toddler out of mischief. I mentioned to some other mothers that we could take care of each other's children a few hours a week to allow each of us some freedom. But my innocent idea was not met by smiles that would have reflected the beauty of the

surroundings. The concept of solidarity among women was as yet
nowhere on the horizon, certainly not on the one bordered by the
Glarner and Wäggitaler mountains and Lake Zurich. In retrospect, it
seems that we all had to prove to each other that none of us could be
replaced by someone else in our role as mother.

Those women had everything, or so I thought. Security on a
political and financial level, a network of family around them, roots,
a healthy life in beautiful and orderly surroundings. What made it so
difficult then to be friendly and outgoing? Why was it they could not
live WITH one another but insisted on living NEXT to each other?
My own insecurity, however, was such that it interfered with my
judgment of the situation. I felt it was I who must be doing something
wrong; I coiled up in my shell, hurt and misunderstood.

Our second son was born and I was kept busy and happy watching
them discover their world. I wanted to be a good mother and give
them everything I had not had – roots, security, warmth, enough space
to grow. Yet, I don't think I was altogether content; there was this bit
of me that yearned for a mental challenge. With no nurseries or
playschools until the children start kindergarten at the age of five,
there was little I could do in the way of a job. I started to give private
lessons in English at home. A year or so later this effort developed
into a part-time teaching position at the community college in the
next town. There I could work evenings when my husband was at
home to look after our boys.

I recall standing in front of my class of fifteen women who had
left the security of their homes to learn English with me one evening
a week. Getting my books out of my briefcase, I came across a
magazine on women's issues I had brought along for a colleague. As
it was the first of its type in Switzerland, I thought it might interest
them, too, and held it up for all to see. "Is that something 'feminist'?"
one of the fifteen inquired. Without waiting for my reply, she
addressed the class: "We don't want anything like that, do we?" The
other women nodded their heads in agreement or were silent. Their
reluctance to inquire into new ideas in no way reflected the openness
that meets the tourist when he travels through this beautiful country.
I was disturbed by their negative attitude, and I asked myself the same
question that has puzzled me ever since I came here: "Why is their
outlook on life so rigid? Why will they not even find out what the
new ideas contain?"

In spite of these challenges, the teaching experience was successful enough to give me some of my self-confidence back. I started thinking about creating a playgroup for Michael, who was four. I did not understand or heed the warning that this new idea would bring me 'nothing but trouble.' I could see only positive aspects. The group got under way, to the pleasure of the mothers and children who shared the experience.

Some weeks after we had started, I received a call from a woman who wanted her little girl to join. I explained to her that this meant she also would have to participate as we mothers took turns working with the children. She liked the idea and agreed to come. However, it was not long before the phone rang again. "My husband won't have it," the lady said, crying. "Since the boys hadn't had a playgroup," her husband had argued, "why should the girl? And anyway, didn't she have enough to do around the house?" He also objected to his wife joining any group of which Mrs. X was a member – the Mrs. X who was "bossing everybody around" (including himself) on the church board.

Another similar incident comes to mind. I had been upset for some time over the very dangerous exit from our school, where in the winter the children would slide down a little slope right into the road. There are no school lights or speed bumps or any other safety regulations around the school. A serious accident was, therefore, only a question of time. Strange enough, the other mothers who were as concerned as I was, did not support me in getting the authorities to act. The usual answer was a hunching of the shoulders accompanied by "they do what they want to do anyway." The 'they' were the politicians who seem to be in office not by the votes of people like themselves, but somehow through an act of God that could not be questioned. The various parties involved referred the problem to a still higher 'they' over which they had no jurisdiction. A gate was eventually installed, but only after my indicating that I would submit an article about it to the local newspaper.

I had not got involved in the issue because I had wanted to "make myself important with it," as my neighbor reproached me a few months later. Neither had it been my intention to "organize people," or "run everything." My work in the playgroup and my teaching activities were also interpreted as acting against traditional feminine ideals. If my actions had left the wrong impression, how could words convince my neighbor of the opposite? I was stunned. I was devastated. It was a long time before I was able to let this painful scene resurface in my memory, before I could bear to examine her accusations objectively.

A few years after that confrontation this same neighbor came to ask me for my signature on a referendum in favor of a common start of the school year in Switzerland. Oblivious to her past argument against female involvement, she explained to me – in what appeared to me my own words – how important it was that everybody accepted responsibility for the community. She herself was working part-time in the old people's home and was feeling better than she had for years. My bewilderment was complete. What had moved her to change?

Was it simply a question of time? Had I overrun her with my ideas? I had been fortunate to have the opportunity to meet people of different backgrounds and life styles in America and England, whereas my neighbors had never even moved out of their Canton. Maybe I had also not given enough thought to the great differences between these societies. I had simply expected that ideas could easily be transposed from one country to another. I certainly had not realized that foreign ideas – as constructive as they might be – had to go first through a process of adaptation in order to be acceptable.

I can now understand that my neighbor's anger was because my participation in a playgroup and my part-time job seemed to show that women were not necessarily 'predetermined' to spend all their time at home and that compromises could, indeed, be found that were not harmful to a woman's home and family. I had disturbed her convenient attitude that women cannot and need not bring about changes because "they have not time." She stamped 'feminism' and 'emancipation' as bad words because they implied change. As "l'homme est le chef," she did not have to be responsible for her own life or for anyone or anything outside her own household. Having learned that it is better not to ask too many questions, I will unfortunately never know what had moved her to change camp.

* * * *

Because of my husband's job, we were able to return to the USA for two extended stays. With the children at school all day, I took the opportunity to enroll for courses at the local universities. This experience, together with the distance, gave me a new perspective which helped me to understand that a large part of my difficulties in Switzerland were not so much due to me personally, but resulted from a clash between the traditional values of Switzerland with the more cosmopolitan ones I had picked up in America. This realization did much to soothe my hurt feelings. And later, when we were back again in Switzerland, it made me less defensive. I no longer felt offended when my neighbor preferred to look intently into her laundry basket rather than notice me on the other side of the hedge. It gave me the strength to be once again the first to shout a cheerful *"Grüezi"* across our differences.

The experience at the university also gave me a new awareness of how much support women were indeed able to give each other in so many different ways. And if I eventually completed my college degree at the ripe age of 40, it was largely thanks to the unwavering support I got from my women professors and fellow women students. I felt myself to be part of a common struggle – the struggle of balancing the roles of student, mother, lover, cook and chauffeur. For the first time I came to appreciate this sisterhood of women, and I have been looking for its existence ever since – on both sides of the Atlantic.

Beautifully costumed, complacent, immaculate, imperturbable, poised, passive, serene and demure Swiss dolls. Photo SNTO.

The first incident that comes to mind in Switzerland happened at the local supermarket on a horrible Tuesday some months ago just before noon. My son Michael was due home for lunch in a few minutes and, rushing to transfer my purchases from the counter into my shopping bag, I dropped the eggs. Of course it was not the small box but the one with the dozen! The assistant who was called to clean up the mess gave me one disdainful look before proceeding to mop up the eggs. I could understand that, with lunchtime closing only five minutes away, I had upset the entire routine. But my apologies remained without an echo. I felt like a naughty child caught in the act. How could I have been that clumsy? I looked around for a sign of understanding from the other women shoppers – a tiny smile perhaps – that would show me I was not totally inhuman, that this accident could have happened to them also. No, their faces portrayed no such possibility. It would NEVER happen to them. I thumped my food into the back of the car, and in my anger, locked the car key into the trunk. *"Typisch Frau,"* I heard the man say to his wife as he got into the car next to mine. There were nods of agreement over my stupidity, but no smile, no offers of help from his wife or the woman parked on the other side of me. Empty looks again. Fortunately, I found someone in the nearby garage to open the car for me.

One of the interesting things about the feeling of sisterhood is that you always know immediately when it is present. You also know when it is absent, as it was that day. But I do recall its magic presence at another supermarket, this one in Harrison, NY. It was on a Friday, around 5:30 p.m. at the Shopwell cash register. In my usual hurry, I had left my wallet with my money and check-cashing card at home, something I only realized when it came to paying. The cashier had already rung up my order and the cash register would remain blocked until I paid for my groceries. Without the slightest trace of irritation, she just leaned back on the counter and pleasantly told me to go over to the supervisor for help. The line at this time of day was long, but still the woman behind me told me to relax and "Don't worry, dear, it has happened to me, too." The other faces further down the line were also not drawn taut with frustration but seemed to accept human imperfections as a fact of life. I was angry with myself but was saved the pain of feeling ostracized.

As regards friends I have had a long time, I have experienced 'sisterhood' everywhere I have lived. The same applies to women who meet to share a common interest, such as a language course, a gymnastics group, or a pottery class. It seems easy to be supportive of other women one KNOWS in some way, as if sharing one interest assumes a common basis in other respects also. In these circumstances, there is little disparity. But what about when women meet as strangers – on a bus, in a doctor's waiting room – where support is granted solely and spontaneously because there is some form of immediate trust and intimacy based on our shared experiences and commonality of purpose? When trying to recall such situations, I remember many smiling faces: some black, some white, some Asian, a few Swiss, but most of them American. Why is it, I asked myself, that sisterhood – so widespread on the other side of the Atlantic – grows so sparsely in this mountain climate?

Is it a question of need perhaps? In America, the early settlers – both women and men – could not have overcome their hardships without relying on the help of strangers. Having left behind the secure network of family support in their originating countries, women were forced to reach out to strange women in order to survive. The experience has, I believe, shown the American woman that she can, indeed, make it without a large family to fall back on for help. This in turn freed her from the boundaries of the clan and oriented her towards other women – an orientation which laid the seed for 'sisterhood.'

In Switzerland, however, certainly in this typically rural part, the traditional family with all its cousins and nieces, aunts, great-aunts and grandmothers used to provide the necessary support for physical and social survival. But with more and more farmland turned into housing estates, the large family is increasingly losing its basis of existence. Social mobility becomes a requirement forcing the traditional families apart. Isolated in an apartment or confined in the fenced and hedged-in garden of a one-family house, the Swiss woman of today clearly needs the interaction with other women but her traditional up-bringing has not only left her in the false belief that she "does not need strangers," it has also not taught her how to reach out to strangers. I recently saw an advertisement in the local newspaper where a young woman living in an apartment block with her two children was looking for another woman to share some interests. What a round-about way to glimpse through the sparkling white curtains into another woman's home!

This attitude of "not needing" help from outsiders is compounded by an almost innate distrust of strangers. The only way I can interpret this is that for many centuries anyone from beyond one's own valley was considered a potential adversary. The threat of being overrun by strangers was always there. And, of course, this fear persists. Only now the threat is not physical but directed against the homogeneity and highly-prized identity as members of a closed group. It takes the form of a foreign work force and of 'city folks' moving into villages, destroying the feeling of security "where everybody knows everybody else." It is not the ground for spontaneous interactions.

America, on the other hand, has been spared the threat of being attacked from just across the valley. Its people have not needed to become defensive. Except for the small minority of native Indians, everybody could be classified as a foreigner. People of many races, traditions and cultures came to live in the same land, making it necessary to be tolerant and open to what is new and different. (Also, immigrants, almost by definition, were more the type of people willing to accept the risk of change and confrontations with strangers.) Women were forced into contact with women who not only wore different dresses, but spoke different languages and had different values. Except, in the areas where the Indians lost their fertile fields to immigrants, the newcomers did not oust natives. The ground to be worked on was new to all of them, and women who moved in later did not necessarily threaten the existence of the present population. There was plenty of space for everyone, plenty of space for 'sisterhood' to take root.

The educational system in America represents this principle of tolerance by emphasizing the development of the individual. Like all systems, it has its flaws, but on the whole, American children come out feeling good about themselves. The sheer thoroughness of the Swiss educational system does bring forth a well-trained and well-disciplined work force, but at the expense of spontaneity and creativity. It does nothing to enhance an individual's belief in his or her potential. The system also is still geared to a division in roles and, as a consequence, women come out believing themselves to be less capable of great things than men do.

Such an educational system and the general attitude it fosters do nothing to give women a belief in their own potential, both as a worker and as a person. Is it surprising then that many of them lack the self-confidence and self-esteem to reach out to other women? Confused about their possibilities, these women use words like 'Feministin' or 'Emanze' to slander other women, words which in

German have only negative connotations. Before sisterhood can develop, there must be trust in oneself as an individual. Only then is it possible to be tolerant and accepting of others. But this trust is defined by the soil and by the climate. 'Sisterhood' cannot grow without the right conditions.

The overemphasis on role behavior still ruling Swiss society with an iron hand further aggravates the trend already set at school. It does not free a woman to share whatever talents she possesses. Forced into a role, she comes to share a common martyrdom instead: suffering the restrictions of being a woman is made only bearable if other women suffer the same restrictions. It is hazardous to leave this coziness of a majority, when acting on one's private beliefs is coupled with loneliness. It takes a strong personality, indeed. I, for one, have often found myself wavering between standing up for what I believe is right and conforming to the Swiss norms because I also would like to 'belong'.

* * * *

I was on the train to Zurich last week. The lake passed by in its picture-postcard beauty, the serenity of the few boats taking in the light breeze was contagious, and I couldn't help smiling at the woman across from me. But it dissolved as she looked through me at an advertisement on the wall. The woman on the other side of the carriage studiously carried on knitting, no smile of mine would break her concentration and inveigle her to share the lovely moment. A few seats down the aisle, a young girl, the clean-American-student-type, looked my way. I chanced another smile and was rewarded by one in return. The lake was beautiful again.

Waiting to get out of the train, I stood in front of her in the aisle, so I asked, "Are you American?"

"Yes," she answered, "but do I look that American?"

"It's partly that," I said, "but what really gave you away was that you smiled."

"That's funny," she said.

"No, it isn't," I answered.

* * * *

I do not doubt that Swiss women will become more liberal and outgoing. Social and legal improvements for girls and women are bound to be made which will lead to less undermining of womanhood, femininity, female power or whatever it is called. The structure of society will change as Swiss women are exposed to different life styles by the media and by 'foreign' residents. An emphasis on equal job opportunities for boys and girls must also lead to achieving a greater consciousness and respect for individuality. And this, I believe, will lend women the necessary trust in themselves to reach out and to share. And, I hope, to smile.

Heidrun West. Photo A. West.

A Taste of Home

by Tony Obrist

While walking from the aircraft to the terminal building at a Swiss airport with the other passengers on a plane from London, I was startled by a noise of breaking glass just behind me. When I looked round I saw a woman passenger staring disconsolately at a most unsavoury looking mess on the tarmac. Mixed up with it were fragments of glass, one of which still carried a label which identified the broken bottle as having contained HP Sauce. Her paper Union Jack carrier bag (whose printed slogan "I'm Backing Britain" was sadly ironic in the circumstances) had proved unequal to the weight of goodies the lady had crammed into it, and the handle had torn, dashing the sauce bottle to its doom on the tarmac.

This was in the days before scampi, avocados and pasta had hit British cookery – when an Englishman's idea of *haute cuisine* was a good plate of good solid food doused with the said sauce, a fiery, dark brown concoction whose composition would have been summed up by the Cook in *Alice* as "pepper, mostly". The famous bottle was to be found on tables in every restaurant and boarding-house and almost every household in England, including that of Mr. Harold Wilson, the Prime Minister. (For Scotland I cannot speak.) Now, slopped on the airport tarmac, the stuff looked even more disgusting than it did on food.

And yet my heart bled for the poor woman. How carefully she had selected this delicacy to carry back to Switzerland! Had she planned to bring joy to the soul of a fellow British expatriate housewife? Or to introduce sceptical Swiss friends to a new culinary delight? Or was she, selfishly, intending to hog the whole bottle herself over the coming weeks? Be that as it may, her dreams lay shattered on some corner of a foreign airfield.

Every expatriate longs for one or more items of his (or, as in this case, her) native food unobtainable in the country of exile. For my unknown fellow-passenger it was HP Sauce; for other Britons it is pork sausages, or sliced steam-baked white bread, indistinguishable from cotton wool by the uninitiated. In my own case it is Black Magic chocolates, their manly taste and assorted hard and soft centres so different from Swiss *Pralinés*, which are filled only with fudge in various shades of tan and are made from such rich ingredients that you feel sick after eating three.

My hand trembles as I type. Of course, when I say Black Magic, Dairy Box would do at a pinch, or even Milk Tray ... My address can be obtained from the Editor. Thank you very much.

Excerpt from the Anglican Church of Basle Newsletter for June 1988:

CONCERNING THE BAZAAR

The summer holidays are almost upon us with the "migration" to (and from) Britain. While you enjoy yourselves, please nevertheless spare a thought for our Christmas Bazaar in just 6 months' time. If you and your friends travel by car, here are a few suggestions how you could make it another big success. We would be grateful for "heavy goodies" such as Golden Syrup, Lime and Ginger marma-lade, Mango Chutney, Mincemeat, Jellies (lots!), Bovril and Marmite (jars as used in normal families not in institutions!), Tea and Custard Powder. All these sell well.

We hope that those travelling by air can still find a corner in their suit-case - or even pocket - for the odd jelly!

Föhn Within

by Mark Morrison-Reed

My parents had four children – all born in Chicago and raised on an unremarkable but nice tree-lined street on the city's southside. My father, a chemist, was awarded a fellowship from the National Research Council to pursue his work at the University of Berne for one year. That summer, of 1962, we packed our bags, rented our house and left for Europe. This was going to be an adventure.

We disembarked in Le Harve and took a train to Paris. It is not easy to travel with your parents when you are 12 and 13 years old as my brother and I were. In fact, it was a trial. My brother Philip and I always made sure that we walked as far away from the rest of our family as possible. You would find us either way in front or far behind our parents and two younger sisters. We hoped that people wouldn't notice that we were with them. We tried to act cool and mature as we strolled along pretending we knew where we were going. After all, who would think that these two young Afro-American boys were with that Afro-American family thirty feet behind?

Philip and I simply didn't want to look like refugees. Our mother always looked like a refugee. She could never manage to pack just one suitcase for each of us. It felt like we were carrying everything we owned. There were suitcases of all shapes, sizes and colors, plus shopping bags full of other stuff. She brought crackers and cheese, fruit and candy, paper towels, toys and other nicknacks, and an extra jacket or two. She always looked disheveled and lost, and of course had our two younger sisters in tow. It was just too much for agonizingly self-conscious teenagers to bear. We kept our distance.

When we arrived at the French-Swiss border in Basle, Dad got out to change some money in the train station. But then, after only a few minutes and before he had returned, the train suddenly started to move forward. Mother bolted up from her seat and in a second had the compartment window open. In her mind she must have imagined herself, with her feeble German, four children, a thousand pieces of luggage and no money, heading into Switzerland while her husband would return to find the platform empty.

She leaned out the window, her arms flailing. She began yelling frantically in the little German she knew. *"Halt! Halt! Mein Mann! Mein Mann! Halt!"*

Any Swiss who happened to hear her must have thought her husband was abandoning her. At that moment abandoning her seemed like a great idea because I was ready to die of embarassment.

"Oh, Momma, be quiet!" we whispered as we tried to tug her back into the compartment.

When she kept right on yelling, "*Halt! Halt!*" Philip and I rushed out of the compartment and down the corridor seeking a place to hide. As it was, the train soon came to a stop. It had just been pulling forward to the Swiss side of the border.

We arrived in Berne the day before 1st August and moved right into a three-storey apartment building on Finkenhubelweg. This street, if you can find it, runs parallel to Stadtbachstrasse which borders the railroad tracks as they converge on the Hauptbahnhof. Narrow, little Finkenhubelweg deadends into a horse stable at the bottom of a hill. It was so wooded and quiet that you never felt like you were almost in the center of the city. We entered the yard through an arch cut in a cave-like hedge. Only then did we see our new home. A pale yellow stucco building rose before us. It was a long walk up to the third floor, and remained so. But the apartment was bright, airy and spacious.

The typical cloud formations of the *Föhn*, a local wind which blows with rage. This photo was taken of the Jungfrau region. Photo SNTO.

What we children found most exciting and frightening, when we dared to get close to the edge, was the big balcony from which we could see much of the city. On a clear day, when the *Föhn* blew in we could see every detail of the Bernese Alps. The notorious *Föhn* is a warm, gusty wind that roars over the mountains from the south. It isn't just any wind. When the *Föhn* is blowing, many of the Swiss can be heard complaining about how it makes them feel, but it also makes the Alps look like they were right behind the Gurten, the mountain that stands above the capital city.

Switzerland truly seemed like a wonderland when, from the balcony on our second night, we saw the world exploding before us as the Swiss celebrated the anniversary of the Helvetic Confederation. Indeed, Berne became an enormous amusement park for Philip and me. We visited the bear pits, and all the museums around Helvetiaplatz. We were enamored with the wave machine at the swimming pool until we discovered we could float down the River Aar on inner tubes. We found a fireworks shop in the old town. Many hours were spent marvelling at the toys at Franz Carl Weber on Kramgasse near the 'Zytglogge'. We gorged ourselves on chocolate. And we had never experienced anything like the *Zibelemärit*. In Berne in late November they have a huge street party to celebrate, of all things, the harvest of onions. The crowds filled the main streets which were closed off to traffic. Young people danced, yelled and formed long lines in which they snaked their way through this giant confetti battle. Philip and I were exhilarated as we wandered about the old town watching the people, throwing confetti and eating marzipan, candy and hot chestnuts.

Winter came and we took up skiing. No sooner had we learned how to snowplow, than we wanted to start ski jumping. So we fashioned, out of snow, a one-foot-high ramp. Philip, who was fearless, went first. I, always the more cautious, couldn't resist following. We couldn't stop but it didn't matter since we fell down most of the time anyhow. We'd spend the day on Gurten or take a postbus to Schwarzsee. We were rarely home if we didn't have to be. Such freedom we had never known back in Chicago.

In fact, in Chicago I had become a prisoner in my own house. During the last two weeks before we left I was too terrified to go outside. On the last day of school as I walked out of the door, an older boy, a high school student, picked my report card out of my pocket. With it was a transfer to the school I would be attending in Switzerland. I tried to get it back but gave up when it became clear that all I would get was punched-out. After all, it was just a piece of paper and a copy could be obtained easily enough. Besides it was my last chance to walk my first girl friend home. When we were about a block away from school, I noticed a gang of boys approaching us from behind. I thought nothing of it. Then someone yelled, "That's the nigger that's going to Switzerland. Let's kick his ass." Suddenly someone grabbed my shoulder and swung me around. As I raised my arm to hit him, the blows of a half dozen black teenagers knocked me to the ground. My glasses flew off. They kicked me and ran. My nose was bleeding, my face swollen and my shirt ripped. Worst of all my friends had all fled. After that, I all but refused to leave our house. A few times before we left I crept out the back door and slipped down the alley to visit a couple of my friends. And right before we departed I walked past my girl friend's house – on the other side of the street. I waited for several minutes in front of her home. But I never saw her again. Switzerland was like a rebirth for me. Fear evaporated, and I could live again.

Life was good and for the first time it felt like it was my own. I was a thin, gangly youth. I wore thick dark-rimmed eye glasses and had a little nose they kept sliding down. Behind my glasses lay my big cheeks and quick smile. I was a nice kid turning into an awkward adolescent, and becoming more self-conscious as one does at that age. The way some of the Swiss reacted to us only made this sense more acute. In Switzerland we were a real curiosity. People would stop and stare. Unabashedly some would even ask to touch my baby sister's hair. We thought it was quite rude. But what was intolerable was when people would point and say, "*Neger, Neger!*" Philip and I were always ready to fight when we heard because it sounded like "Nigger" to us, and we weren't going to put up with it. Mother would proceed down the street, dragging us along by our wrists, while she explained that they weren't really calling us a bad name. They were just surprised to see Negroes in their country. She said we were "exotic and unique". We had a hard time believing her, and we still thought it was rude to make such a big deal of our color. We developed an instinct for knowing who it was that wanted to stare at us and found our own methods of dealing with these overly curious individuals. They would pass us by not yet daring to look. My brother and I would begin our countdown. One, two, three! Together we would whip around and stare right back at the person who was inevitably gawking at us. We loved to see the embarrassed look on their faces.

This experience was balanced by the hospitality of those who knew us as friends and neighbors. Frau Tobler, the wizened but kind widow who lived in the first floor apartment, doted on us. She liked to have us to tea. But before our mother let us go down she would drill us on good manners like how to say *"danke schön"* and *"bitte"* and how to hold a tea cup properly. Frau Tobler would serve us in her sunny parlor. Everything was perfectly laid out. The table was covered with a lace table cloth and set with a china tea set. We sipped tea and snacked on cookies and little chocolates. Although frail and bent, she would shuffle about getting whatever we wanted, just like our own great Aunt Irene would have done. We could not help but feel good, even as we struggled to communicate in German. We talked about school and she talked about her middle-aged son, Walter, who she hoped would marry someday.

Our father's colleagues and their families were generous with their time. One couple took us mushroom hunting. The hunt was fun. The surprise was that we enjoyed eating those "nasty things" we had always avoided: other people showed us the important sites. We romped around the newly excavated Roman theater near Avenches. We liked the battlements at Murten so much we went back several times. There we learned about the Battle of Murten where the Swiss Confederation defeated the Duke of Burgundy. But besides those of Dad's colleagues and Bernhart, an older boy across the street, we did not have much contact with Swiss children our own age. We preferred hanging out with the other Americans we met. When we were with them the thing to do was to make fun of the Swiss. We complained about everything: the weird food, the lack of American conveniences and particularly the Swiss rules and formalities. Our mother wouldn't listen to our complaints. She put it in perspective by saying that we looked to them as strange as their habits looked to us. She suggested the situation called for tolerance.

The Swiss certainly noticed us, which was flattering, and they did regard us as "unique and exotic" like mother had insisted. They also made efforts to help us, although their curiosity was often more evident than their goodwill. In time we could laugh at the ways some of the Swiss people responded when they met us.

"Where are you from?" A man would ask.

"Chicago," I would reply.

"Oh Chicago in Africa?" he would say.

"No, in America."

"In South America?" He would return.

"No, in the U.S.A." I'd say.

"Ahh-Soo, I understand. Chi-ca-go! Gangsters! Gambling! Al Capone!" And then he would make like a machine gun. "Da da da da!"

Sometimes the ignorance was not so humorous – and action, not tolerance, was what was needed. Loeb is a large department store at the head of Spitalgasse across from Bubenbergplatz, right in the middle of Berne. One day as Mother was walking by Loeb she noticed in one of its show windows a display of American products. In the middle of this display was a large picture of some little coal black children eating watermelon. They were sitting on the steps of a run-down shack with wide eyes, big grins and juice running down their bellies. Well, Mother had a fit. She called the U.S. Embassy and complained. She took the wife of a professor, one of Dad's colleagues, with her to translate and went down to the store. She told them it was wrong to foster a stereotype of Afro-Americans as little "black piccaninnies". The offensive picture came down.

The first six months we lived in Switzerland, Philip and I attended the English Speaking School of Berne. It was housed in a narrow two-storey building on Thunstrasse. The school had four classrooms and eight grades. The student body was largely made up of the children of diplomats, so naturally the school offered French as the foreign language. Living in a German-speaking part of Switzerland, I naturally wanted to learn German. They tried to teach me French but I successfully refused to learn it.

Sheila was in the eight-grade class with me. I no longer remember exactly how our friendship began. Behind the school there was a little yard where we congregated during our breaks. Everyone would stand around and talk since we couldn't leave the school grounds. Somehow she and I moved through that first awkward stage and discovered that our attraction was mutual. We would linger in the yard at the end of recess. Eventually there was a furtive kiss while standing in the stairwell. I blush when I think about it. Her skin was pale and her dark hair hung half way down her back.

Sheila lived in Muri near Berne, a well-to-do suburb where many of the U.S. Embassy personnel lived. Her father was the Military Attaché. I went out to see her one afternoon in late fall. The day was gray and brisk but it did not matter as we walked around talking and holding hands. It was getting dark early so we hid deep in the shadows of her back yard and kissed for a long time. The sensation was new and totally absorbing. I can still remember her hair.

I asked her if she would go to a movie with me the following week. Sheila went in the house to ask. I sat on the stone wall that enclosed her yard waiting. When she finally came out of the house I could see her father standing in the doorway. She looked at the ground as she approached me. The conversation was short.

She said, "My father says I can't go to the movie with you." She paused. "And I can't see you anymore."

My stomach sank. "Why?" I whispered.

"He won't let me go out with you because you're a Negro."

"What?" I said.

"Because you're a Negro," her voice trailed off.

We stood there for a moment but there wasn't anything else to say. She turned and left. I watched and then slipped over the stone wall.

I walked slowly down the Muristrasse toward the train stop. I was cold inside. Rubbing my hands, almost pulling at the skin, I looked at their reddish brown color. I couldn't change what I was. Feeling all at once rejected, unloved, angry and then aware of the unfairness of life, the protest mounted in my mind. "It's not fair! It's not fair!" A shell closed around me. The train took me home.

We were learning that, while the Swiss naiveté led to embarrassing and sometimes annoying situations, it was some of our countrymen, at the U.S. Embassy, that caused us the most pain. My sister Carole, who was in the 4th grade, also attended the English Speaking School. One of her classmates was Robin McKinley, a frail little girl who was chauffeured to school in a limousine. She was the Ambassador's daughter. When her birthday came around she planned to have a party in the briefing room of the Embassy where there was a movie screen. There were going to be American cartoons. Her whole class was talking about it and everyone was invited except Carole.

I had a good friend, Ralph, whose father was the Second Consul in the United States Embassy. One spring day he invited me to come play softball against a team from the U.S. Consulate in Geneva. The opposing team took to the field first.

I hadn't yet batted when I heard some white fellow – they were all white – yelling from the outfield. "What's that nigger doing here?"

I froze. I would have disappeared if I could. But there I was, a friendly but timid 13-year-old and here was some man calling me a nigger. Ralph was furious. The next thing I knew Ralph was dragging me onto the field so we could fight this guy while I was trying to drag Ralph off the field, trying not to make a big scene. Years later I realized that Ralph was right. We should have fought. Instead, my fear, shame and hurt overwhelmed me. I retreated, my head bowed, my hands in my pockets and tears in my eyes.

A year had passed and the time to return to Chicago was approaching. But I had a different idea. I had visited a boarding school in the Bernese Alps. It was called the Ecole d'Humanité. I had fallen in love with the place. I had gone so far as to ask for an application form to the school. And after writing the essay required of each applicant I gave the form to my parents and told them to fill it out. I wanted desperately to stay and go to the Ecole. I was enamored with my life in Switzerland. If I never returned to Chicago it would have been fine with me. My parents consented. I assumed it was an easy decision. It had not been. But they had not burdened me with their reservations.

August 1st came and went. This time we were prepared for the celebration with an arsenal of fireworks on our balcony.

When we began packing to leave there were all kinds of things that needed to be returned to the friends that had lent them to us: bicycles, skis and skates. We had also borrowed a sled from my friend Ralph and so in mid-August I headed out across the city toward Muri to return it. I felt rather silly on the bus in the middle of the summer, dressed in shorts and holding a sled. People stared but that was fairly normal. I stepped off the bus and started up a path that led to his house. The path crossed a big field. Coming toward me were a father and his two young sons.

My Swiss German was not very good but I could make out what he was saying: "Look, there is a Negro. He comes from Africa. He is looking for snow. He doesn't know any better."

As they proceeded past me I nodded and greeted them in my best Swiss-German with, *"Grüessech mitenand."* I laughed all the way to Ralph's house.

It was time for my family to leave Berne. My parents were worried. My brother Philip was trying not to cry. They later told me that he was devastated. He and I were born a mere 13 months apart and had been raised a bit like twins. We had gone everywhere and done everything together for as long as we could remember, now he felt abandoned. It took years before I understood his reaction. But as they drove away I felt more free than sad. Finally and happily, I was on my own.

* * * *

I took the train. From Berne it goes through Thun and then Spiez. Interlaken always made me nervous because the first time we had gone to the Ecole we'd mistakenly gotten off the train in Interlaken West instead of Interlaken Ost. Philip then asked if this was our stop. Realizing our mistake we frantically threw our luggage, skis and ourselves back on board. I had always felt more confident when I traveled with my brother.

The train proceeded to wind along the shore of the Brienzersee. In Meiringen the train switched to a cogwheel locomotive to climb up the Brünig Pass. The postbus was waiting there and began its 9km traverse of the Hasliberg. First it goes through a deeply shaded, mossy, boulder-filled wood that has always seemed to me to be enchanted. One comes out of the forest suddenly and sees across the valley as the bus hugs the narrow road that has been blasted out of the rocks. Below is the River Aar rushing straight down the Haslital in its man-made channel. Across the valley the Reichenbach Falls surge over the cliff and above it all towers the massive wall of the regal Wetterhorn and its attending peaks the Mittelhorn and the Rosenhorn with the Rosenlaui Glacier lying before them like a carpet. When one lives on the Hasliberg, this is the scene one's eyes always return to - the Wetterhorn resting high above the Grosse Scheidegg. I still carry that view in my heart.

The Ecole d'Humanité is in Goldern, the next to last stop the bus makes. The Ecole is a progressive, international, co-educational boarding school. For me it was utopia – a very primitive and demanding utopia, but none-the-less paradise. We lived in a cluster of seven mostly old weather-worn buildings, and a few houses scattered throughout the village. The oldest of these swayed and creaked when the *Föhn* howled against them. When the winds were silent one heard the underlying rumble of the 130 students: the constant murmur of voices through thin walls, the giggles and squeals, the thud of feet racing down sagging stairs, and swoosh of behinds sliding down banisters, the crashing gong to tell us when to get up and when to eat. The life style was spartan, the fare simple, the responsibilities many, the classes informal. Hard work was one of the Ecole's distinguishing features: felling trees, chopping wood and the occasional finger tip, hauling coal, keeping fires going, shovelling snow, and helping the local farmers during haying time. And there were girls. Girls that liked me. How I loved it all.

The student body was international, although largely western European. There were Swiss, Germans, Americans, British, Dutch, Scandinavians, French, Canadians, Yugoslavians, Arabs, Israelis and Central Americans. My one roommate was a Swiss boy named Philipp, and the other a German named Jörg. We usually got on well. Living in this isolated and idyllic community, race seemed like it was of no concern. In such a cultural jumble of people a friend was a friend, and a fool was a fool regardless of nationality.

Back in the United States on August 28, 1963, right before I arrived at the Ecole, over 250,000 people had participated in the civil rights "March on Washington". I had followed it in the INTERNATIONAL HERALD TRIBUNE. Two weeks later, after school had begun, four young Afro-American girls were killed in the bombing of a church in Alabama. It became a ritual for me to go to the library, which also served as a classroom and dining hall. There I would spread the HERALD across a green formica table. The light by which I read came in through a bank of windows that faced the serene Wetterhorn, but I had entered a different world as I hunted for articles about the USA. Sitting there I would read about demonstrations, protests, and sit-ins; beatings, murders and race riots.

My mood swirled about like the *Föhn* that had uprooted the forest on Schwarzwaldalp which sits beneath the unmoving Wetterhorn. I would read it but I could not believe. It seemed like it must be fiction but I knew it wasn't. I was confused. I was torn. I felt guilty living with the knowledge that other people were suffering and dying, while I was doing nothing. I thought the world outside must be crazy. I wondered if the Ecole was the only sane place. Who could I talk to about my inner turmoil? Who would understand? I didn't speak of it, nor could others sense the pain hidden behind my gregariousness and laughter. No one guessed how alone I sometimes felt.

The tension in me mounted. What was real? How could we be so untouched by the world? In the Ecole we all went around acting like race was of no consequence. People would say to me, "I never think of you as a Negro." This was an observation I never quite knew how to take. Or someone might comment, "Oh, I forget about your color."

And day to day we were so busy that I too would forget. But the stranger's stare would remind me; so too the newspaper articles. And something within myself would not let me forget for long either.

One day, I made a poster and began marching around the school protesting some non-existent discrimination. Soon I was joined by others in my mock conflict. That same day the parents of another American student were visiting. The father, Reinhard Bendix, was a noted sociology professor at the University of California in Berkeley.

He and his wife were walking up the road toward the school when they looked up and saw me coming toward them – running from a swarm of students yelling, "Get him! Get the nigger!"

As we ran past the professor called out, "What's going on?"

"Oh, we're having a race riot," came the reply as we rushed on.

They were so stunned that to this day they can recall this moment when they first saw me.

The whole thing had gotten out of hand. And now I was more conflicted than ever. For me there was no enjoyment in our game. The word "nigger" even said in jest was jolting. The make-believe race riot left me feeling depressed.

My protest, and there was a real protest going on behind the acting out, was to call attention to my blackness. The trouble at the Ecole was that in our efforts to be "color blind" in how we treated one another, people were ignoring a fundamental part of me; that was aside from certain stereotypes. Some people assumed I could play basketball well, which I could not, and sing Negro spirituals, which I could, and dance, at which I tried very hard.

They also tended to typecast me in school plays. I was always Kaspar, the Moorish king, in the Christmas play. In Shakespeare's 'The Merchant of Venice' I was the Prince of Morocco, one of Portia's failed suitors...

Bowing, I would bid her farewell: "Portia, adieu. I have too grieved a heart. To take a tedious leave: thus losers part."

"A gentle riddance. Draw the curtains, go. Let all of his complexion choose me so," was her comment as she watched me depart.

No matter how many times we played that scene I always felt rejected. But it passed quickly because truth be known I wasn't crazy about THIS Portia. Actually with the females at the Ecole my color sometimes worked in my favor.

Every Sunday evening the entire school gathered in the big hall for *Andacht*. It was a devotional hour spent listening to stories, thoughtful readings and quiet music. On one such evening Frau Hirzel, an opera singer from Zurich and mother of one of the students, came to entertain us. She serenaded us with songs from many cultures.

I was sitting toward the rear of the hall. My mind was elsewhere. My attention was caught when I heard her say. "Und now I vill sing a Negro spiritual."

I listened. She began to sing in her operatic style. It seemed strange to me. The flowing, soft, melodic tones were missing. The beat seemed too much like a march and the voice was forced. But for me it became comic when I listened to her German accented English.

She sang, "Vade in da Vater, Vade in da Vater Child-rren. Vade in da Vater. God's going to trrr-ouble da Vater."

I was trying to contain a chuckle when the teacher next to me, Herr Poeschel, rolled his eyes and gave me a quick little grin. I lost it. I was laughing uncontrollably when I noticed that Herr Lüthi, the director of the school, was looking over his shoulder directly at me. His lips pressed tightly together, his eyes stern and eyebrows raised meant unmistakably, "Control yourself!"

I froze or at least tried to. The best I could manage was not to laugh out loud. But my chair shook and my eyes teared until she finished. Thankfully she sang only one Negro spiritual.

It is a tradition at the Ecole d'Humanité for everyone to take a six-day hike in June. We were returning from that six-day hike. Goldern was a long sixty minutes away. We set out from Meiringen, heading up the mountain. Anxious to get home, our group strode quickly up the trail. Our clothes were dusty, our faces grimy and we smelled like cows, But that's normal when you've been hiking for six days and sleeping in alpine huts at night.

I was marching up between my two friends with whom I'd helped lead the hike. Our pace was fast and determined. When we passed the Schrädli, a cluster of three farm houses, we knew we were already half way there. Around the very next turn in the road stands a large wall. Right there the path narrows. In this tight place stood, staring, his mouth agape, a little boy. As we came closer he turned and ran, crying *"Mutti, Mutti!"* I can no longer remember exactly what he said, *"Der Schwarze kommt,"* or *"Ein Neger!"* But it was immediately clear that he was scared and fleeing from me.

I cried out the lines I had spoken as the Moorish king in the Christmas play, *"Fürchte dich nicht*."* And then *"Hab keine Angst*,"* but he ran even faster. Whether it was some story he had heard, or some primal fear of the unknown that drove him, I'll never know. But there was no doubt that he was terrified. My heart sank as he ran crying to his mother.

My head hung. I felt miserable. And once again I was wishing that I simply wasn't there. It may seem strange but I felt that I was somehow guilty, although I had done nothing except to be there and be black.

He reached his mother. She stretched out an arm, then slapped him across the face. He whimpered as she dragged him to the side of the road. I glared at her as we marched past in silence.

A rage began to build in me. How could his mother dare slap him instead of embrace him? And why should I have to feel bad about what I am, and the color that is my birthright.

In that moment I saw that something was wrong with the world and not with me. From that feeling came a realization: the world must change!

I think it was then that I began to try. We marched on, I looked up. Ahead the forest thinned. The meadow appeared.

Mark Morrison-Reed as teenager and today.

*   *Fürchte dich nicht* and *Hab keine Angst* both mean 'Don't be afraid.'

The Hausfraus

by Barbara Bruzgo Higelin

We see each other about once a month. The meeting places vary: the park playground, the pool, each other's homes, but the main activity is always the same. We talk. Over coffee, over the heads of children demanding attention, over our current knitting or needlework project, we talk.

We first became acquainted as English teachers while working together in one of Basle's many private language schools. When we met again, years later, we had all become mothers and we found we needed these get-togethers to talk to each other in a way we could not talk to our Swiss neighbours. We all speak German fluently enough to get by, and one of us has even become very proficient in Swiss German. So speaking English together is not the main reason we meet regularly. We need each other to exchange ideas about child-raising, something we all have difficulty discussing with our Swiss friends.

The topics are as varied as we are. We might discuss someone's discovery of a new regional attraction, the latest English film now playing at the cinema, where to find a good jazz dance class or the merits of various Basle playgroups for pre-schoolers. One thing is certain, the conversation will inevitably include reflections on our lives in Switzerland.

"It happened to me again yesterday," says Brenda, mother of a teenager and a five-year-old. "I started talking to one of the mothers at school about the documentary on TV the other night about child labor and she gave me that blank look. You know what I mean? The one you get when you talk about something that doesn't fall within the neutral territory of what you're making for lunch and what you use to clean your kitchen floor. That look always makes me stop in mid-sentence. I can see her wondering why on earth I'm talking to HER about something like that."

"Oh yes, that helpless, mindless female role that drives me wild," adds Jeanie, feminist mother of two little girls. We laugh remembering her story about working on a school project with two other mothers whose only reaction to each new problem was to bemoan the fact that there were no fathers nearby to solve it.

"The playground mentality of 'Do unto others as they've done unto you' is my biggest problem at the moment," comments Candice, mother of three pre-schoolers. "When someone hits one of mine on the head with a shovel, it goes against all my upbringing to tell mine to hit back. In England mothers just don't do that."

"For me it's the lack of response I get when I complain about something like the school system. It's like talking to blank walls. Nobody even defends the system. They simply look at me as though I've stepped on forbidden territory," complains Janet, our Swiss German specialist and in our view the best integrated of us all. "I have no idea if they even agree or disagree with me. They seem to have no comments about topics like a child's having the same elementary school teacher for four consecutive years."

"But that's how they are about ANY problems they may be having with their children," crys Katy, mother of two particularly mischievous little girls. "You'd think I'm the only person on the block whose kids draw on the walls or get into my make-up!" Heads nod all round.

"It seems to me," adds Candice, "that mothers around me all have model children who never cause any problems, even though I can SEE that's not the case! I know their children have temper tantrums or wake up during the night because I've seen and heard them doing those things. But whenever I bring up a problem I'm having, everyone smiles at me and says they've never had that problem. They also seem to feel free to give me a lot of unsolicited advice on how to discipline my three – I would never dream of telling them how to raise their children!"

"Well I sure wish MY neighbor would give ME advice on keeping my house spotless," sighs Katy. "Her kids are the same age as mine and she doesn't even have the breakables put away! Whenever I'm invited over there for coffee, I spend all my time grabbing things from Allie's hands or reminding Terry to stay at the table so she doesn't get crumbs all over the place. I can go over there at 3 in the afternoon on a day when there's no school and the place is impeccable!"

As working wives we had lived in small apartments. As mothers we needed living quarters with more space. When we moved from the relatively impersonal atmosphere of an apartment into the more suburban chumminess of house-living, we encountered some basic cultural differences that took us by surprise.

"I didn't realize I was expected to invite the neighborhood women to MY house for a get-acquainted coffee," reminisces Jeanie. "Where I grew up it was always the neighbors who welcomed the newcomer. What a surprise it was when the one woman I had befriended very diplomatically explained it to me! I'd been wondering why I'd been getting the cold shoulder from everyone else."

Candice lives in a complex of two-storey apartments which open onto individual gardens and a central playground. She remembers, "At first, the neighborhood children would simply walk right into the house and start looking around, without even knocking! I put a stop to that quickly. But I still have some problems with the older children. Often when I ask them not to do something, like asking a 10-year-old not to sit on the toddler's tricycle, they ignore me and go right on doing it. They pretend they don't understand my German. And I swear I'm the only mother in the whole complex who gives other people's children snacks! Sometimes there are children I've never seen before asking for things to eat!"

Sometimes our idle chatter together allows us to get over upsetting encounters with Swiss neighbours. Those initial lumps of indignation in our throats often turn into laughter.

We chuckle at Brenda's story of her neighbor's offer to clean the under-sides of her window sills.

Janet tells us her neighbor has been silently protesting against their cat by depositing all the cat droppings found in her yard on Janet's doorstep. Heads shake in disbelief.

Katy gets advise almost daily from her neighbor about things like how she should sweep up the dead leaves "before they stain the tiles on your patio."

Strangely enough, we become quite defensive whenever we encounter criticism about the Swiss from 'foreigners' such as family or visiting friends who do not live in Switzerland.

"I can live with a once-a-week wash-day or without a clothes drier, but I would find it hard not to be able to let my children play in the backyard for fear of their being kidnapped."

"My children are both completely bilingual, and I'd hate for them to lose that."

"I like the absence of color racism. My kids have school friends of all sorts of exotic backgrounds who have been adopted by Swiss families."

"When the new baby was born, the local women's club sent me a woman who helped out tremendously cleaning, cooking and taking the older one out for walks. Later when I began working part time, I found a day-care mother through them who took other people's children into her home during the day. Day care back home is much more expensive and less personal."

"When I see my sister's children who are almost the same age as mine, they seem to have grown up too fast. Her oldest is a cheerleader and her biggest ambition at the moment is to make it into the 'in' sorority at her senior high. I'm glad my kids don't have that kind of social pressure here."

"My American magazines are full of articles about things that seem to me to be almost ridiculous, like sending your baby to a gym class or going jogging with your toddler to make sure she gets enough exercise! Here my kids spend hours on end running around outside playing!"

"And television! I'd hate to have to compete with all the programs available on TV back home! At least here there aren't so many of them. My 12-year-old nephew in the States has his own TV, telephone and computer and hardly ever comes out of his room! Somehow it's easier to say no to that kind of thing here, even if the neighbor's kids have it."

"I find it easier to say no to lots of things here. My friends back in the States are always going gung-ho over the latest fad, like teaching your baby to read or raising your kids according to someone's newest method. Here I don't feel pressured into doing those kinds of things by my friends and neighbors."

"Recently my teenage daughter asked why I'd told someone I wouldn't want to raise children in the States today. I tried to tell her about the high school drug scene from my own teaching experiences 15 years ago. I could see she thought I was exaggerating. She's never been exposed to anything like that here. Just think! It was 'only' grass then – now it's cocaine!"

"Back home I'd feel very uncomfortable now being a full-time mother. There's so much pressure on women to work. I enjoy being able to be at home and watch my children grow up without feeling guilty about it."

We begin to gather up children, toys, and the English books and magazines we've exchanged. As we head home, snatches of conversation float on the fog.

"I can't believe it's already winter again! Six months of gray skies!"

"I mustn't forget to get some milk. The fridges are so small here!"

"Boy, did I miss the bread when we were on holiday."

I wave goodbye, thinking how glad I am they're around. Without them I might not have adapted so well to living here.

Watch Those Wicked Words

by Stanley Mason

The first time I ever ventured on to the Continent from my home in the depths of Britain was when I went to teach at a school on the Zugerberg, a hilltop in Switzerland, in the late thirties. I got out of the train at the valley station of Zug, and what did I see? A small tram standing in the sleepy square before the station with a big placard in its window that read: *Zugerberg hell*.

I very nearly turned tail and fled, once and for all. I even suspected that the placard might have been put there by some diabolical pupils who were not particularly interested in having a new English teacher. How was I to know that in this case *hell* only meant "bright", and that the purpose of the placard was to tell the townsfolk under a blanket of mist that the sun was shining up on the nearby heights?

Sometimes I wonder whether the same thing doesn't happen to other travellers. For instance, what do people think who journey by rail to St. Moritz, only to stop in a station with a big sign saying: St. Moritz Bad? I suppose everybody knows that St. Moritz isn't so bad after all and decides, even though with an inward tremor, to go ahead and take a chance. But are they so sure when they go to Bad Ragaz?

I feel even more deeply for expectant mothers who, turning the corner of some small Swiss station, are faced by a notice bearing one brutal, laconic word: *Abort*. After all, wouldn't "WC" serve the purpose just as well?

The reader will notice that we are here on delicate ground, straight among words that offend our most intimate sensibilities. But there is no remedy: these words exist and are in use, if only in foreign parts, and we therefore have no alternative but to face them with whatever fortitude we can summon.

If a man called Fuchs gives his name to a flower, or a pianist by the name of Charlie Kunz rises to fame, the Anglo-Saxons get round it as elegantly as they can by the expedients of pronunciation. The flower becomes a few-sha and the pianist a Coonds. But when you go to live near a town called Scheidt, and it proves to be pronounced in a way that substantiates your very worst apprehensions, there is simply no way of getting away from it. This evil fate befell a friend of mine from Gloucester through no fault of his own, and he tells me that in the early days of his sojourn in the area his voice used to break with shame every time he went to a railway ticket counter to ask for a return to Scheidt.

The Swiss of 'Big Basle' went to considerable trouble to tease those of 'Little Basle' back in 1640. They erected this gilded mask with clockworks to make the tongue stick out for 15 seconds and the eyes roll back and forth for 45 seconds. A newer version of this figure with his rude tongue can still be found looking over the Rhine today. A newcomer to Basle may not only be shocked by the seemingly wicked words heard in Switzerland but by this wicked monument as well. Photo SNTO.

In the same way the Dutch may be seen to wince when anybody
mentions the name of Zurich Airport, and the Germans when they
first hear the opposite of the simple English word "before".
English-speaking visitors to the Locarno region are also shocked to
see the initials of the Ferrovie Autolinee Regionali Ticinesi writ large
on the local buses, and I once heard a Canadian murmur that he had
never seen anything quite as big and blue as that in his own country.

The worst trick a malicious fate can play on you, however, is to
give you an impossible name. I was once called in to help a Swiss
acquaintance whose brother had died in the United States, so that as
next of kin he had to handle correspondence about the estate. My
acquaintance was called Schittli, which is a very respectable Swiss
name. His brother, strangely enough, had a different surname. Having
emigrated to the States, he had discovered that the family monicker,
however respectable in Appenzell, just would not do in Pittsburgh.
He had therefore had it changed to Hittli, which involved only the
sacrifice of two consonants. Alas, it was not long before the shadow
of one born in Braunau fell over Europe. Hittli was so near to Hitler
that the parallel became, for an immigrant, decidedly uncomfortable.
Poor Hittli took the only course of action open to him, and sacrificed
a vowel. He died a Hattli.

One's first confrontation with these wicked words from foreign
tongues may easily come at a tender age. I happened to belong to the
generation which experienced the introduction of the so-called
"modern" pronunciation of Latin into English schools. Previously the
Latin word *jam*, for instance, had been pronounced just like its
English counterpart, and this had enabled us to invent such sentences
– admittedly not in the best classical tradition – as *Caesar adsum jam,
Pompeius aderat* (Caesar 'ad some jam, Pompey 'ad a rat). As fate
would have it, the word used to represent the First Declension of
nouns in our grammar book was *causa*. This word had hitherto
seemed innocuous enough, as the first syllable was pronounced just
as in the English word "cause". With the advent of the new
pronunciation, all that was changed. In the Genitive Singular there
was already *causae* (cow's eye), then came an ominous suggestion
in the Ablative, and finally the catastrophe of the Accusative Plural,
causas. One of my more genteel fellow-pupils, when asked to repeat
the First Declension in class, came to an embarrassed stop after the
Vocative Plural. He could not bring his well-bred lips to utter the

fateful word. There was a terrible silence, in the midst of which came a hoarse whisper from a back row: "Say 'cow's bottom', you fool."

Lest any reader should suspect at this point that the writer of these lines might take a perverse pleasure in citing all these unfortunate instances, let me assure him that my sensibilities are no less easily offended than his own. When a German-Swiss acquaintance of mine pointed out a passage in an English novel where lovers were described as "lying among the furze", I did not as much as smile, although he himself broke out into the coarsest of guffaws. Much the same happened when an Italian I knew first heard an American call his girlfriend "My pet". I thought the Italian would choke with mirth but I kept a straight face. (I realize of course that these two points may be lost on persons not conversant with German and Italian, but I feel sure they will prefer to be spared the obnoxious truth.)

On one occasion, however, I must confess that I allowed myself an indulgent smile. A young man from Yorkshire who had come over to the Continent to do an apprenticeship was returning to England. On the day of his departure he proudly produced a ticket issued by a Swiss mountain railway and showed it to me. On it was indicated the price of one trip.

1 *Fahrt* Fr. 6.50

He was taking it home to Yorkshire to prove to the locals just how high the cost of living is in Switzerland.

In the Swiss Army

by Roger Bonner

I open my desk drawer and pull out a folder entitled 'army'. Inside is a gray booklet with the French inscription *Livret de Service*, in German *Dienstbüchlein*, pasted on the cardboard cover. The label is yellowish and dirty. My name on it has been smudged and the typed AHV or Social Security number is fading. Yet this 'Little Book of Service' in its harmless, nondescript appearance will be with me most of my life. A passport can be renewed, issued in another streamlined form; the 'Little Book of Service' defies all change. My father's was the same, and if I ever have a son, his will be the same.

The 33 pages are divided into various sections, some scrawled full, others empty. One section is headed: *Résultat de l' examen de gymnastique,* a physical and sport examination made on November 4, 1965, in Olten, a German-Swiss town.

* * * *

It was chilly in the long school corridor. Young men were filing in, bumping into each other, joking nervously. Robert could barely understand the Swiss dialect. His palms were clammy and he wanted to run away. But there was no escape, not from the law, not from the police enforcing it. At twenty-two a man is eligible in more than one way. The government wants you. In his case two governments. These gawky, pimply boys shuffling into a waiting room were reminiscent of another scene a few months earlier in Robert's life:

May 28, 1965

Selective Service System
Local Board No. 140
San Diego County,
San Diego, Calif. 92101

Dear Sir:

Your request for a personal appearance before your local board is acknowledged.

We have made an appointment for you to appear before your local board at the address given above at 10:10 a.m. on June 10, 1965.

"Think you'll get out of it?" A guy in a tight blue suit and tie nudged him. They were all dressed as if waiting for a job interview.

"I've gotta," Robert answered. "I'm objecting."

"Me too. What's your grounds?"

"Well, I'm Swiss...from Switzerland...and we can't do military service for another country. But I grew up here and want to study."

"I'm studying now and I'd like to continue," the guy answered, tugging on his tie. "Christ, I don't want to get my ass blasted off in Vietnam."

When Robert's name was called he jerked. His stomach burned. A man was motioning to him from an open door. He entered what looked like a converted dining-room. Several men in civilian clothes sat around an oblong table. Most of them had crew-cuts, and the one at the head wore a checkered shirt. Facing Robert behind the table was a portrait of Lyndon B. Johnson grinning down implacably.

"Oh God," he said under his breath. "I'm a goner."

As an alien resident he was eligible but he had been able to leave the States legally before they drafted him so he wasn't a real draft-dodger. But now in Olten there was no way out. This time the Swiss wanted him, for seventeen weeks of military training, what they called *Rekrutenschule*, school for recruits, a rather harmless boot camp when compared with the mounting death tolls in Vietnam, wasted villages, napalm, choppers whirring over jungles and men scrambling for their lives.

"Kleider ausziehen," a young lieutenant shouted.

Robert soon realized that could only mean "take off you clothes." Some snickered as they were herded into a locker room. Shirts and pants dropped. The air grew musty. Robert was thin and gangling; he had a stooped posture from hunching too much over desks. He squinted through his horn-rimmed glasses at the row of huddling flesh and thought of a Prussian story where young intellectuals were degraded. It was like Boy Scout camps, or high school gym showers. Someone was always laughing, shoving...

"Next!"

After their being examined like cattle, they put on tracksuits and went outside to run and jump. A lieutenant clocked their time with a stopwatch. Robert received special attention because he could not speak German. Already the others were calling him '*der Ami*'**.

** *der Ami*, the Yank.

Robert didn't really mind. There were advantages, he noticed, in not always catching all the words.

When this part of the recruitment was completed, they were given a written IQ test. The lieutenant came and told him to finish a story in English. Then they had to sit around and wait again. Some mumbled that the Old Man had arrived, the Colonel. The last phase would consist of a brief interview where you could state your job preference in the army.

"*Übermittlungssoldat, Artillerie*" he repeated to himself. That's what he would request.

This brilliant idea had been on the advice of his well-meaning relatives from a small farming village near Solothurn. Robert's father had left home at a young age to become an engineer. After he married, his Geneva-based company had sent him off with his wife and two children to California. Robert was seven then in 1951 and so only vaguely remembered vacations where a hoary blacksmith grandfather picked them up from the station with a horse and carriage. Then the shadowy forms of aunts welled up, and bullying cousins up to such pranks as squirting milk at each other with cow teats. Uncles appeared too, one with large ears.

It was sixteen years later when Robert returned the first time to Switzerland with his mother. A delegation had been waiting for them at the station to drive them to the village, now by car. Uncle Wilhelm stepped forward, beaming from a ruddy face, his ear lobes dangling like tiny gorged leeches. His plump, freckled wife Vreni kept raising her hands in amazement. A cousin lumbered up to him and gave him a crushing handshake, then he sized him up with a smirk. Robert was all spruced up in a suit and tie, his hair pasted down with brilliantine.

Later they made the rounds of more relatives. The village lay at the foothills of the Jura in a verdant valley dotted with dozens of hamlets. It was farming country, but a watch factory nearby had given rise to a cottage industry. A steel factory on the main railway network also provided jobs. The villagers were staunch Catholics, set in their ways. On Sundays they all went to church. Afterwards the women went home to cook and the men congregated at the local inn. No change it seemed had taken place in hundreds of years, except for television and cars.

Aunt Marta was the most fervent churchgoer. He dimly recalled a huge, one-legged woman. She had had an accident when young — a plow cut her foot; gangrene had set in and the leg had had to be amputated. Her farmhouse was a low dwelling with a broad roof. The barn was attached and only a narrow corridor separated the living quarters from the stables.

The barn was cool and reeked of cow dung. At its end a pig grunted and squealed. The outhouse was still there, and Robert remembered as a boy passing what then appeared to be a giant sow snapping and grunting at the boards of her pen as he inched by to relieve himself.

They rapped on the living-room door.

"Come in," a voice bellowed.

She was sitting, almost quaking on an oven-bench, covering her face.

"Gaston, Gaston!" she wailed. She still called him by his first name, a French name he had dropped in the States because the kids at school had incessantly teased him with 'gassy'.

Robert tentatively went up to her. She latched on to him, yanking him down with powerful arms to her mighty breasts, hugging him in a firm grip, rocking, wailing. He gasped for air. Her clothes were permeated with that odor of animals and food that hung in the entire house. After releasing him, she pulled his head to her face and with tears streaming down her cheeks, she planted kisses on his forehead and mouth. Two or three bristles sprouting from her chin stung him. He wanted to wipe his face.

His mother, a small, dark woman, stood helplessly in the background. She was next, and bravely succumbed. Then other relatives emerged from the kitchen, though more restrained in their emotional outbursts. There was cousin Heidi, blond and stocky, with two sniveling kids tugging at her apron. Fritz, her husband, wiry with a broad gait and a suspicious handshake. Alphons, his uncle and husband of Marta, looming, gaunt, taciturn with a secret twinkle in his eye. They encircled Robert and his mother, plying them with questions in a vociferous, crude-sounding dialect. He only grasped the meaning of bits of it. Suddenly they were in collusion, huddling, whispering. The name 'Hans' was murmured. That was his father. His parents never got along and had separated. His father had returned several years before to Switzerland and his mother had never wanted to reconcile. But Vietnam had changed all that. Now they had decided to try living together once more.

Aunt Marta was wailing again, alternating between wrath and pity. Hans was her brother, and she knew him well from childhood

days, that despicable scoundrel! She nodded as Robert's mother
recounted a harrowing tale of drunkenness and threats, then she raised
a meaty fist and pounded the table, uttering the name 'Hans' over and
over again. His mother piled on details, fired by familial support.

"That Hans!" Down went her first and an entire canon of Catholic
condemnations. "That Hans!" Her brick-red cheeks were about to
burst.

After the storm broke and abated, the subject turned to 'poor
Gaston' and his future, more exactly his impending military service.
It was then that his aunt waved for him to come once more to her
bosom.

"You're such a fine and gentle young man," was the gist of what
she said. "So delicate!"

Fritz and Uncle Wilhelm stood on either side, grinning with a
secret relish. Only later did he find out that the army in Switzerland
was popularly known for toughening sissies. You went in a boy, you
came out a man. That was the significance of those grins. But the
women were genuinely concerned and fussed over him, promising to
send the traditional parcels of extra food and chocolate. Aunt Marta
vowed to knit socks. Then she couldn't restrain herself and reached
for him, pulling him back to those breasts.

"Listen, Gaston," she whined this time. "When they ask you what
you want to do in the army, say '*Übermittlungssoldat*'. That's just
the thing for a fine boy like you – a radio-operator!"

It seemed the grins on those men's faces broadened just a trifle.

* * * *

The young lieutenant came up to him and said in broken English:
"You come. Now we go to colonel," stiffening at the mention of that
name. "In here."

They entered a conference room. At the far end was a desk with
a grayish man sitting erect in an impeccable uniform. His cap was
adorned with broad bands of gold indicating his rank. The lieutenant
only had a slim gold line winding around his cap. He rushed up to
the colonel and briskly saluted, then said something inaudible. He
motioned for Robert to come forward. Other lower-ranking officers
were standing about, peering at him, and one corporal in baggy pants
with some papers in his hand. Robert was in a convivial mood. All
the special attention made him feel important. He casually ambled

right up close to the desk and bent towards the colonel whose eyes suddenly widened as his jaw dropped. The colonel leaned back against the chair as if he wanted to push himself through it, then raised his hand in a gesture of helplessness. The lieutenant was instantly at Robert's side, grabbing him by the arm. A buzz of animated talk came from the others.

"Sree meters," the lieutenant gasped at Robert. "You must stay a distance away of sree meters from ze colonel." He pushed him back to the correct distance.

The ruffled colonel quickly regained his august composure.

In German he said, "So you are the American," glaring at him in mock severity, exchanging smiles with the other officers.

Robert feigned ignorance. "I don't understand German," he said in a broad accent.

Obviously the colonel couldn't speak one word of English. He faltered for a second, visibly embarrassed at this moment of exposed weakness. The lieutenant rushed up to him and translated.

"Da colonel vants to know vere you vish to go."

"To go?"

"Yes, vat part of ze army."

"Oh, yes. Transmission," Robert answered with pride. And I want to serve with the French-speaking troops. I know a little French."

He escaped one real war and found himself in a most strenuous, but bloodless one.

The colonel nodded and the others nodded. The corporal sat scribbling over documents.

"So," the colonel said in a gruff voice. "You want to be an *Übermittlungssoldat*. Do you understand me? And be sure to learn German. A Swiss soldier must know the language of his country!"

Everyone agreed. He was led out of the room.

* * * *

I pick up my *Dienstbüchlein* again. In Swiss-German dialect it is called *'büechli'*. The Swiss-Germans have a penchant for diminutives. By adding the suffix 'li' to almost any noun something small and sometimes cute results: *Blüemli, Vögeli, Küssli* – like saying in English flowerlet, birdie or kissy-wissy. So I page through this 'Little Book of Service' filled with the terms of war, weapons, orders, examinations and other red tape. On page 4 the words *Apte au service, Diensttauglich* have been stamped in bold type meaning I am physically fit for military service. My career can begin. For the ordinary male citizen it is a career that will span 30 years. The Swiss Army is a militia, ever ready to mobilize in case of war or a national emergency. Its soldiers take their rifles and gear home with them, including live ammunition. After the *Rekrutenschule* they must serve a total of eight *Wiederholungskurse* (WKs) or 'repetition courses', one lasting three weeks for each year. If any WK is missed, then taxes must be paid. Until the age of fifty a few sporadic courses follow amounting to a few weeks. At fifty a soldier returns his rifle and equipment to the army and is then assigned to Civil Defense until he is sixty and his military career ends.

Popularly these courses are called *Bundesferien* or government paid vacations. Some men look forward to this time because they can get away from work and their families, see old buddies, and drink and carouse. Sometimes for the wives it is also an opportunity for a *Seitensprüngli*, a 'little jump to the side', a minor infidelity. For others still who are upwardly mobile, a rank in the army is an indispensable stepping stone for a career in industry, government and finance.

Art. RS 23 Stelrm. Bttr., Bière 31.1 - 28.5.1966. My little book is a perfect record, testifying in the minutest detail that which time would otherwise have erased. If I decipher the abbreviations they state that I did my school of recruits in the artillery in a place called Bière for seventeen weeks in winter. That was 21 years ago. I have never been back to that village in the French-speaking Canton of Vaud. It looms up in my memory as a wide plain with numerous barracks and even more taverns. It is time to go back. The month is July. It is hot and sultry, and I am going back...this time voluntarily.

* * * *

He had been waiting for days for the *Marschbefehl*, the march order. He was living in a small room let to him by a distant relative who was an invalid and deaf in one ear, but of a wonderful disposition. Annie was her name. The situation had grown unbearable at home. His father had reverted to his old habit of going out for a pack of cigarettes on Friday evening and not returning until Sunday afternoon, half-sober, without money, and belligerent. On one such occasion he had threatened to shoot Robert with his army rifle. In Switzerland the cases were rare when these weapons were used for crime, but they were handy for threats. Still, Robert was not taking any chances.

One day Annie knocked on his door and handed him the mail. It was there, stating in official terms where and what he was to take along. If the order was not observed, the matter would be turned over to the police. Legal threats were universal.

His mother, worn and haggard from worry, accompanied him to the station. She was trying to live again with his father, this time in Trimbach, a town on the outskirts of Olten.

"Don't worry," Robert comforted her. "It'll be over soon and then we'll leave. I'll get a job."

He had no profession, no training, just a high school diploma that was not acknowledged in Switzerland.

"Write soon." She held up her hand to wave. Then the train slowly pulled out.

He leaned back in the seat to watch the wintry landscape smear by. It was a clement winter with little snow. Gray patches were scattered over the fields. He looked down at his timetables. He had to change trains at a place called Morges; he was worried he might miss the stop.

* * * *

I stand in front of Morges station. It is a bit shabby and run down. The sun is brooding behind clouds, making the air muggy. A motorway is just off the rails down the embankment. Cars flit up a ramp, past tower buildings. In front of the station the town sprawls in a jumble of concrete down to the Lake of Geneva. Sometimes you can see a shred of blue, but today mist is hanging over it like a dirty sheet.

Across from the main railway line there is a narrow-gauge train waiting. Its two cars are painted a bright green with the initials BAM written across the sides. I get in and it starts clattering up the hill, past those blocks, past neat suburban homes with comforters hanging out of windows to be aired, then suddenly a countryside of hills and vineyards, lush grass and ripening wheat. Vufflens-le-Château is the first stop. The towers of a castle appear from a hill, striding forward like giants as the train continues.

After half an hour Bière comes into sight at the end of a valley flanked by hills. There is no sign of a military base. A snug station house, farmhouses, a crumbling fountain dated 1895 and the words *Les Trois Sapins*. Bright red geraniums hang from its sides. I had forgotten the fountain. The narrow streets winding up to the sleepy village. Only a distant popping sound, like boys shooting off firecrackers, gives an inkling of something more.

* * * *

Several corporals were waiting for them on the platform, shouting in German and in French. The train on the way to Morges had swelled with boisterous young men, singing, laughing. Only Robert felt lonely and sat apart. But the crowd made it easy for him. He only had to follow them. And when they all pushed and shoved into the small green train, he knew this was the last stop.

"Over here!" A lieutenant had appeared and was gesticulating.

The French-speaking had automatically grouped together and were making sly remarks about the German-Swiss. They felt strong. It was their turf.

"Over here. In two rows! Fall in...fall in." Later such an order would coalesce an entire battery. Now it only fostered chaos as the men stumbled about.

"We're going to march to the barracks," the lieutenant piped at the top of his voice. "This way."

They trudged along the main road leading up to the post office and the town hall – "La Mairie". Some people had lined up along the side, calling to them, pointing. Two pretty girls in thick jackets smiled and this caused a minor pandemonium of whistles and yells in the ranks.

"Come on! Hurry up." A corporal brought up the rear.

In about ten minutes they came to a site where rows of barracks stretched, obscuring a wide plain visible through gaps between them. An arsenal was firmly planted at the entrance to a courtyard. A military truck rumbled out towing a cannon. When they reached the mess hall, they made a sharp turn into a square.

Here the buildings were dark with small high windows. Some soldiers were running from one end to the other and crawling on their bellies under parked vehicles. They passed by and came to an open space where three buildings stood. The middle one had a clock-tower perched on top. It too was dark and grimy. Bare trees, like claws, jutted out from the tarmac. They stopped in front. Two tables had been set up and some officers waited behind them.

"Stand along here," a sergeant said, motioning to them. "In one long row. Come on, you too over there!"

"*Appel*," (row call) another... one bellowed. "When your name is called out say 'here'."

Someone screeched 'here' in a falsetto voice, and there was muffled laughter.

After the row call was terminated they were divided into groups of twelve and assigned to their respective corporal.

A tall, lanky man strode up to them. "O.K. Come over here. I'm Corporal Gérard. Have we got all of you? Good. Now you just do as you're told and we'll get along fine...*compris*? Follow me into the barracks."

They climbed up worn stone stairs into a gloomy interior. The wall plaster at the base had been kicked loose. There was a musty smell of leather, sweat and oil in the air. They went down a long corridor past rifle racks and chipped, battered doors.

"This is your room," Gérard said, kicking open the last one. A wide room with a large window at the end gaped at them.

Steel-framed beds with shelves and cupboards next to them were on both sides. In the middle there was an elongated pine table with benches. But what stood out the most was the floor – it was pitch black.

The corporal led them in and when each had picked a bed, he went into a locker-room type of speech, the kind a football coach likes to give, with hand chops in the air.

"You, over there," he snapped, startling everyone. "Wipe that silly grin off your mug! As I was saying, you'll learn what the army is all about. That goes for each and every one of you...*compris?*" He always ended his tirades with that word.

Robert took the opportunity to examine what fate had tossed his way. All these youths of different size, personality and background in a culture that he was still trying to understand. Who would be a friend, who an enemy? Any group represents a cross-section of humanity. Already he could discern the bluffers, bullies, the students and workers, the businessmen, bureaucrats, the conceited and self-conscious – they were waiting to reveal their natures.

They started unpacking their bags. Robert took out a sweater, the socks Aunt Marta had knitted for him, some vitamins his mother had slipped in, his toilet kit, a pair of suspenders. The last item had been specified on the march order. It made him think of Westerns.

"You, over there." Corporal Gérard was to start with that phrase hundreds of times. He walked over to a thin, wan fellow who was undecidedly hunching over his bag, setting aside some maps and a gleaming instrument. "What do you think you're doing?"

"I was just..." he flustered. His thin blondish hair gave him the look of a little old bald man. He knitted his eyebrows and made a grieved expression.

"From now on," Gérard belted out, "you are to stand at attention when I address you. What's your name?"

"Hebe..."

"What did I just say about attention? Are you an idiot!"

"Hebeli." He shifted from one foot to the other and looked at the fingernails of his right hand.

"You are not just Hebeli, but Recruit Hebeli...now say that."

"Recruit Hebeli."

"What a gentle little voice pussy cat has," Gérard taunted. Then burst out: "Louder!"

"Recruit Hebeli."

"LOUDER!"

"RE...CRUIT HEBELI!"

"That's more like it. And then you are always to answer '*Oui, mon Caporal*' whenever I give you an order. *Compris?*"

"Oui, mon Caporal."

"LOUDER, goddamit!"

"OUI, MON CAPORAL..." Hebeli croaked so loud he had to cough.

The others gathered about the bed, some grinning, Gérard turned on them viciously.

"What are you apes gawking at? I want all of you downstairs in ten minutes. Come on...on the double. *Compris!"*

The next few days went on like that, with everyone screaming at them. They were constantly running, running to breakfast, to lunch and dinner. Then there were interminable queues, first for uniforms. As training clothes they were issued old World War II uniforms of coarse, itchy wool. The pants were so wide you had to hold on to them, hence the suspenders. Then there was a cap which had to be worn at all times when on duty, and a long gray shirt that went down to the knees. Combat equipment followed: a helmet with a broad rim curving out on the side, cartridge-belts with complicated straps, leather gaiters with long laces to wrap around your calves, a pair each of hobnailed and rubber soled boots, of leather hard as iron, and finally the *fusil d'assaut* or *Sturmgewehr*, an automatic rifle. There was also a rather quaint *Brotsack*, a bread sack, in which you placed your rations. Regulations always prescribed that it had to be fastened down with a strap. You wore it over your left shoulder, like some Johnny Appleseed ready to sow.

The drilling started every day after breakfast. Corporal Gérard burst into the room at six a.m., screaming *"debout..."* followed by *"allez...allez...*come on...get up...get a move on." Groans and curses came from the beds, then a thumping and crashing.

"In ten minutes you're out washing yourselves....COME ON!"

If you wanted to avoid getting your feet black from the floor you had to slip directly into your boots, then hobble out to the long wash troughs with cold water taps from which you splashed yourself awake. There were no showers in the barracks. That was what had most surprised Robert. Swiss cleanliness was proverbial, yet the recruits could only shower once a week in another barrack, usually on a Friday, the day before their weekend leave.

"Ten minutes more and you're assembled down on the square. Hurry up! Faster...faster..."

Aligning in a straight line was a ceremony, with lots of elbow poking to get the right distance, then you spread your legs in the at ease position, *repos*, and had your hands folded in front of you. Gérard paced back and forth, his sallow face and squinting eyes shooting from one soldier to the next.

"You over there, tie that lace! And you...what kind of a sloppy uniform is that? Did I ask you for an answer? Button...button...aren't you old enough to button a jacket?" And then suddenly he would turn on a victim. "Hebeli...are we daydreaming again?"

"NO, CORPORAL GERARD!"

Robert had already singled out his friends, and enemies. There was Serge, a TV repairman from La Chaux-de-Fonds. Short and stocky, ever ready with the advice of the working world, he was planning to get married and have children. Philip was the only student. A pipe-smoking lover of classical music who had just completed his schooling. He had a distracted look about him and was all thumbs when it came to tying his gaiters and correctly putting on the cartridge-belts. Inevitably his slowness would incur the wrath of the others. In the army everyone is collectively punished for the misdemeanors and shortcomings of the individual. Morin in particular was ready to vent his anger at any given opportunity. He worked in a grocery store in Geneva. Tall, bull-necked with thick lips that always hung open, he loved to push around and humiliate the weak ones, which meant Hebeli and Philip. The rest could ward him off with a curse or punch, but these two were defenceless. Hebeli, an orphan, had been raised by a rich spinster aunt in a fine old house in Lausanne. His greatest passion in life was stargazing. He had taken along astronomy charts and a small telescope. Morin would bully him whenever in the mood, he and his crony Louis, a handsome, swaggering insurance salesman with the reputation of a lady killer. Rumours had it that he was once in prison for some shady deal.

As soon as they were aligned, Lieutenant Wipf, a German-Swiss engineer from Zurich, would come for his inspection. It was general practice to assign a German-Swiss officer to the French-speaking troops, and vice versa. No doubt this was to avoid unnecessary fraternizing, for there always existed a mutual dislike between the two main parts of the country, the French-speaking believing the *Deutschschweizer* to be slow and dull-witted, the Swiss-German speaking convinced that the *Suisse-Romands* were lazy and incompetent.

The lieutenant's ramrod shape appeared from the officers' mess. *"Garde à vous..."* Gérard held his breath as everyone tensed for the word *fix* to snap them up like a taut wire. "ATTEN....TION!"

Lieutenant Wipf, jaws grinding, eyes glaring from behind thick glasses, paraded up and down, then he took over command from Gérard. His first tactic was to run like mad across the square and shout: *"RASSEMBLEMENT"*. The detail of six bolted off, boots pounding the tarmac, helmets wobbling, tugging at the jaw-straps, rifles clunking. As soon as they arrived at the spot where Wipf was standing, arms akimbo, off he would shoot again to another part. And so it went on until they were panting. Then after a short break, Gérard took over to drill them about the assault rifle.

"On you bellies!"

They flopped down on the ground, their helmets beside them, and went through a chanting drill of naming the parts.

"Remove the magazine."

"Remove the magazine," they shouted in unison.

"Hebeli...you idiot! Haven't you learned yet what a magazine is?"

Morin, sprawled out next to him, took this opportunity to slug his arm.

"Yes, you idiot," he spouted. "Don't you know what a magazine is?"

Gérard, grinning broadly, mildly rebuked Morin for interupting his command.

"Unscrew the butt!"

Occasionally a higher-ranking officer came by, a major wearing white gloves. He would test the soldiers. At one such inspection, and they were frequent, this major wanted to view their marching skill. When he barked *"gauche"*, Robert, still struggling with the language, promptly went right, leaving all the others stepping in the opposite direction. This caused general hilarity, until the major's demeanor clouded.

"You." He pointed with one glove in his hand. "Come here."

Robert dashed over, braking at exactly three meters before the seemingly indifferent officer who was gazing up at the trees, hands folded behind his back, foot tapping lightly.

"A VOS ORDRES, MON MAJEUR." He almost blew the major's cap off.

"So." He paced back and forth. "You haven't learned the difference between left and right?"

Robert sweated beneath his helmet as the major came up to him
with a menacing gaze.

"Oui," he ventured timidly.

"What did he say?" the major almost whispered to Gérard.

"OUI, MON MAJEUR," Robert bellowed again. He had
forgotten the *'mon majeur'*.

"That's more like it," the major answered in a mild, almost
pleased tone, then almost bowled him over with a verbal broadside.
"THEN LET'S SEE! Run ten meters to the LEFT...ten to the
RIGHT....LEFT....RIGHT....LEFT....LEFT....RIGHT....I said
RIGHT, *mon dieu!"*

That evening back in the barracks, Robert nursed his feet. The
inevitable blisters were forming on his heels. He had done everything
to soften the leather of his boots, pounding and bending it repeatedly,
smearing in grease, but still his feet swelled and grew rawer day by
day.

Hebeli, or Auntie Hebeli as Morin provoked him, was sitting with
one of his star charts spread out in front of him. Philip was reading a
book by Camus. Two were playing cards, one listening to the radio,
another eating food he had received from home that day. Morin and
his pal had gone out to drink, so there was a brief lull. Robert took
out a block of paper and began writing:

Dear Mother,

Well, it's now three weeks since I arrived in this hell. Next weekend I'll
be coming home on leave. I hope the Old Man is behaving. I think you're
right in going through with the separation, but don't say anything to him
yet. Wait till I'm finished with my service and then we'll figure a way out
of this mess.

You wondered how my 'telephone operator' post is coming along? The
next time I see Aunt Marta I'm going to wrap an entire reel of cable around
her neck! I couldn't have picked a worse job. This week we spent every
afternoon running around in the woods. Me with about thirty kilos of cable
on my back! Someone else runs ahead of you with a long pole called 'une
perche' and hooks the line in the trees. You also have to lay it along the
road and fasten it down with small stakes. This is the foot patrol. I hope
things will improve next week when we move over to the mechanized
patrol with a truck. Because of my language they won't even let me near
a radio. They say the enemy could spot our changing position by listening
to my accent.

Thanks for the package. Army food isn't too bad, but there are no extras...

He couldn't write anymore. He felt like going out for a drink. It was eight p.m. and they could stay out till ten. Lights out at ten thirty. He jumped down from his bed and slipped into black civilian shoes. The band-aids he had stuck on his heels relieved the pain somewhat, but he was worried about the next few days. A night march was planned for Thursday, and military doctors were notorious for their lack of pity. How could he last through it? And if he really went on sick leave, and it was too long, he would have to repeat the whole boot camp.

The evening was frosty and the dirty snow crunched underfoot at each excruciating step. Wreaths of steam came from his mouth, immediately disappearing in the air. The barracks were as silent as boulders crouching behind trees. A light turned on somewhere and a soldier came to the window to toss out a cigarette butt. He walked past the behemoth shape of a truck and a guard stirred. In the distance the village lights blinked like stranded stars. He would go to the Café du Nord. A young waitress worked there that he liked, but she had never noticed him. Still he enjoyed drinking a beer and watching her. Loneliness struck in his chest and he wondered what he was doing in this foreign army. A year ago he had still been in California, just out of high school, and ready to go on to UCLA to study English literature, and now he was among strangers. The future was a blank. He imagined his future self, looking back with smugness, in some profession where he would be successful, where his talent could flourish. But for the immediate future he was afraid. What would he do when the Swiss army training was over? He had worked at odd jobs, such as stacking shelves in a supermarket. From his father he could expect no help.

"When I was seventeen my old man threw me out," his father had told him one evening when they had been back in Switzerland for a week. "I had to look after myself."

He was a practical man, his father, who thought literature was a waste of time.

The Café du Nord reeked of wine and *fondue*. An earthenware casserole of melted cheese, white wine, garlic and a shot of kirsch steamed on a burner. Three soldiers were impaling crusty pieces of French bread on long forks and, one after the other, dipping the pieces in the bubbling concoction. According to custom, if the bread slipped off your fork, you had to pay for a bottle of wine. From a back room came the jangle and beeps of a pin-ball machine. At another table four soldiers were playing cards.

Robert sat at a corner table. The waitress was rushing back and forth from the counter with a tray gleaming with glasses. He liked her firm legs, nut-brown, and slim hips that she swayed jauntily. Her face was pretty with large dark eyes that flashed with audacity. She wore her hair long and its thick lustrous folds bobbed above a lace apron. She had capable hands that firmly clasped the glasses, yet the tapering fingers could also play gently, toy and tease. He so wanted to talk to her, but each time the words stuck in his throat.

She saw him and came over.

"Oui, cheri."

"A beer," he mumbled, looking down so she wouldn't notice his reddening face.

The door banged open and a gust of cold air ruffled the tablecloths. Morin and Louis swaggered in, each puffing on cigarettes. Morin always wore tinted glasses which made his eyes appear smoked. They went over to the card players, Morin bending over one fellow's shoulder. The waitress brought Robert his beer and then went over to the card players. Immediately Louis placed his arm around her waist, pulling her towards him. She demurely removed his hand, tapping him lightly on the chin, and then laughed. Morin encircled her from the other side, but she adroitly escaped back to the counter. She brought back a bottle of wine, and at their continual insistence, finally joined them in a drink. As she was raising her glass, Louis quickly pulled her down on his lap. She squealed and struggled, but he held on to her. Then, bending her backwards, he kissed her on the mouth. She attempted to resist, then briefly gave in, only to push him away, and rise flushed, laughing, pointing a teasing finger at him. The card players and Morin were guffawing.

* * * *

It is after eleven now and I stand in front of the Café du Nord, a square, wood-framed building with a large veranda. Wrought iron tables and chairs are outside, but since a few drops of rain are gradually coloring the pavement dark, no one is sitting there. I enter the smoky room. The same wood panelling on the walls, grimy ceiling. The tables too appear the same, with rickety chairs. The only thing that is different is a wall full of video cassettes with a sign *videothèque* pointing to the back room. The garish titles evoke war and sex. An old man is sitting at the round table near the counter drinking a glass of red wine, staring at nothing. Another man is smoking and reading a newspaper, pausing to slap away a fly. The waitress is about forty, short and stocky, wearing an orange blouse. She wipes her hands and comes over to me. I order a French Kronenbourg beer. A child cries in the back room. The windows are streaking with rain. Suddenly there is a clatter and jingle of bottles. A delivery man is unloading cases of wine and soft drinks. He shifts them across a narrow corridor to the back. A three-year-old girl comes rushing in to the restaurant, falls and crawls over to the old man who looks down and pats her on the head. A moment later her mother dashes in. She is in her late thirties, dark with firm legs, and slim hips, her hair short. I look at her eyes, for some audacious flash, but only irritation gleams there as she grabs the girl by the hand and hauls her off stamping and whining. The window panes tremor as a cannon burst sounds from the hills. These villagers live for the most part of the year with that sound in their ears, the sound of a war that never takes place, that leaves sleeping dogs unperturbed, that makes old men yawn and drowse in their armchairs. I finish my beer and leave.

* * * *

Robert was gasping to catch his breath. Ahead in the dust of the forest road a small army Unimog truck and trailer was bumping and jostling farther and farther away. He cursed Otto, the driver, for his lack of consideration. The cable from one large reel mounted on the truck was unrolling and flipping out onto the side of the road. Two other soldiers were busy securing it there, hopping back on the step fastened to the back of the trailer when they were finished. They had obviously forgotten Robert who had dallied too long at a crossroads with his stakes. His job was to pound them in on both sides with a combination hatchet-hammer and then wrap the wire around them, making sure it lay firm on the ground. At times like that he wished he could wrap the wire around Aunt Marta's neck.

"Hey," he hollered. "Wait!"

The truck disappeared around a bend. They were in a hurry and by the time his absence was noticed it would be too late to turn back. He picked up his hatchet-hammer and remaining stakes and trudged down the road, kicking despondently at some rocks. Distant cannon fire boomed from the hills. The artillery had set up their guns on a plain and they were now shelling the hills. Their job was to establish telephone communication and then hide in the woods. After the battle they had to roll up the wire, but the intervening three or so hours when the war raged were pure bliss. The equipment boxes in the truck were usually amply stocked with wine, bread, cheese and sausages. All they had to do was find a secluded spot in the forest, then camouflage the truck. The rest of the afternoon was spent eating and drinking, gazing up at the sunlight flickering through the branches, finally sleeping.

Robert sat down on the side of the road. The first stirrings of spring were in the air. Tender green shoots began to sprout from the branches. The days were growing longer, making the endless maneuvers, the marches, the drills more bearable. The recruits were also settling down to a kind of routine. The initial gruff manner and bellowing of the corporals and officers had mellowed. Obviously the goal of breaking their spirits had been satisfactorily achieved.

He got up and continued, dragging his feet. By now the truck was probably a mile away. A momentary stillness descended on the forest, occasionally disrupted by distant rumbling. He contemplated his situation. Losing his patrol was not exactly what he needed. But the driver had been at fault. In any event it would mean a loss of face.

He came to a clearing where the forest opened like a gate to rolling hills. The afternoon sun washed the fields with a pale yellow light that ran into the freshly plowed furrows. Crows hopped and flapped away to trees. A path meandered down to a valley and a stream. He stopped in an attempt to get his bearings. The guns sounded again with a dull pom...pom, scattering more crows cawing across the sky. He was hungry and thirsty, and he thought of his patrol holed up somewhere with all that food and drink.

Grinding gears and the throb of a motor made him look up. An army truck was just reaching the top of the hill, then it swayed down, clattering and clunking, tossing its passengers about. It was another telephone patrol. Probably they had laid their line and were also heading for cover. He ran towards them, shouting and waving.

"Stop...stop!"

The truck halted. One of the recruits standing on the back step of the trailer signalled and the truck jerked forward, swerving in his direction.

"Well, look what we've got here," the driver laughed. They were a patrol from the red army, from the enemy.

Robert sat down and laughed. Saved by the enemy.

* * * *

I only have an hour left in Bière before my train leaves. I decide to look for the old barracks. Perhaps they have torn them down. After so many years it is not easy to find my way. Time and memory have played tricks, moving a building from a supposed site, thrusting up a wall I couldn't remember. From the look of the buildings nothing new has really been added. I walk by a square. Recruits are on their bellies with their helmets beside them. They are struggling with the *fusil d'assaut* in the shadow of a corporal making them go through the naming of their rifle's parts. Another patrol passes me. The last soldier is out of step; his bread sack is not properly secured and dangles from his side. A burst of machine-gun fire comes from a rifle range. Some recruits look at me with envy – a civilian. A man who can walk freely, can have a drink whenever he likes, can leave anytime.

I come to where the road divides and still I haven't found the barracks. Then as I turn I see it on the right. Its clock-tower stuck on the roof, making it almost look like a church. But what has happened to the gloomy, dingy, stucco facade? It's been painted now, a light brown. The trees in front are thick with leaves and some soldiers are lined up, tensing for the *garde à vous fix*, and when it comes it breaks through them, and they are rods. I walk away, resisting an urge to snap to attention too.

* * * *

There were two weeks left of the *Rekrutenschuie*. One afternoon they were ordered to assemble on the main square behind the barracks. The entire battery was present. The corporals stood in front of their squads, shouting orders, inspecting uniforms. Then the lieutenants appeared, followed by two captains, a major, and finally the highest-ranking officer, the colonel. He strutted forth, his polished boots creaking, hands folded behind his back. Everyone braced themselves for the command to come to attention. Just at this most awesome moment when all these men clicked into place, Morin passed wind. It boomed, not unlike cannon fire, through the ranks. The colonel stiffened even more, yet he did not condescend to take notice of such a flagrant breach of decorum. Some of the officers whipped their heads through the rows of petrified soldiers, but it was hopeless to spot the perpetrator.

The colonel began in a slow, methodical way, letting his resolute gaze sweep the ranks.

"Recruits," he intoned, jutting his head high. "You are coming to the end of your basic army training. You entered this camp as young citizens, you will be leaving it as soldiers. Your country can be proud of you, as you can be proud of your country."

After fifteen weeks, Robert could almost understand every word.

The colonel went on extolling the virtues of a soldier, calling upon past deeds and future ones. He reminded everyone of the responsibility such a soldier had to bear, what it meant to serve in the army to protect the freedom of Swiss democracy. He went on to stress the importance of discipline and the role of the soldier in private life.

"Next week," he paused dramatically, "all of your training will be put to the ultimate test. You will engage in the final war maneuvers of this basic training. These maneuvers are the closest, hopefully, you will come to war, to actual combat. I am confident all of you will pass this test with distinction."

He raised his right hand to salute and the officers all clicked their heels together and saluted.

"Dismissed," the sergeant roared.

Sleet pelted the convoy of trucks churning up the road through the forest. Inside the soldiers sat dozing with rifles clenched between their legs. All hope of good weather for the last four days of maneuvers was dashed. And they were at an altitude of 1,500 meters. Icy winds lashed mercilessly at them. They had already broken camp, and their mission was to set up an advance command post near the Lake of Joux. The red army was encircling them and they had to break a breach through enemy territory.

Robert's bones ached. His one thought was a warm bed. In the past three days they had only slept three hours, with no relief in sight. He looked around him at the other recruits: Serge on the verge of dropping from the bench, Otto slumped forward, Philip stuffing his pipe. He struck a match and held a weak flame to the bowl, puffing madly, but the tobacco fizzled out.

"Give it up," Robert told him.

"Ah, but I love to smoke my pipe!" he answered, raising his head in a semi-trance. He was so much the French intellectual – indomitable under any circumstances. He had taken along a book by Sartre, and actually managed to read a page or two.

Robert couldn't read anything. He felt sapped and betrayed by this mock war. He was reverting to an animal. The dirt, the camp food, the total loss of culture was demeaning.

They stopped near an embankment where a clump of hewn trees reared ghostly in the dusk.

"We'll set up camp here," Lieutenant Wipf ordered as he scuttled across the slick path.

The soldiers clambered out of the trucks and assembled for instructions. Tents were pitched with straw in them for the night, equipment was hauled out, the trucks camouflaged with pine branches. When everything was satisfactory, thermos flasks of hot tea were passed around, and rationed army cookies and chocolate. Everyone enjoyed the break, soaking cookies in mugs, smoking, making feeble attempts at jokes. From the other side of the mountain the muffled grumbling of gunfire penetrated that brief sanctuary. They all used blank ammunition, so there was no danger, but still the sound was menacing, the situation dismaying.

"Here are your orders." Lieutenant Wipf appeared with a clipboard. A light drizzle of cold rain seeped through the branches. He held a flashlight to the board and began reading off a roster of duties.

"You," he pointed to Philip, "kitchen duty."

Otto was again the driver. Serge had to operate the radio.

"And you," he pointed to Robert. "Guard duty."

The rest received their duties, then the lieutenant disappeared into his tent where the maps were spread. In spite of the turmoil of maneuvers, the platoon was functioning smoothly, being free of trouble-makers like Morin. He had been assigned to another patrol.

Robert went to his tent and flopped down in the hay.

"Just my luck," he cursed. "That means a whole night out in the cold."

He lay back and closed his eyes. A week more and this episode would recede into the past, growing dimmer and dimmer. He would only resurrect it for party talk or for clowning about with old buddies. That was what the army was all about. But now there was this night ahead of him.

In the twilight a jet fighter screeched over the treetops. Had the red army already spotted them? Robert fumbled with his flashlight. Another hour to go before his duty started...

"Wake up! Come on...you're on duty." Serge poked him.

He stood up automatically. In the army all resistance is broken, even that of sleep. He crawled out of the tent into mud. They were on a slope and water was oozing down its side. He strapped on his helmet, threw a raincoat over his shoulders, then climbed up some rocks into patches of moss. It was soft to sit there and an excellent vantage point to observe enemy operations. His duty was rather vague, but he assumed he would just shout when this enemy finally appeared.

The rain had let up again to a light drizzle. He leaned against a tree trunk. The forest was silent, save for the patter of drops on leaves. The sounds of guns too had subsided. Only a tremoring in the earth, as if its belly were rumbling, was audible. Robert could see a field shimmer in waxing moonlight that suddenly spilled from clouds. Then an owl hooted its banshee shriek; something rustled in the bushes, squealed, stopped. He looked at his watch: 3 a.m. He was sure all of them out there were sleeping. Who in his right mind would play war in the middle of the night? Sleep began to lull him, tugging on his eyelids. He would just close them for a moment, perfectly conscious, yet relaxing, actually gaining strength from a sort of meditation...

A terrific crack sounded through the dawn air, as if a branch were breaking over his head. He jerked awake, groping for his rifle that had slipped down on the moss. In front of him an incredible spectacle was unfolding. Tanks were assaulting the camp, blundering and churning their way over the hill like mechanical bulls. Everyone was up and about, dashing for cover. Lieutenant Wipf shouted a retreat. Robert didn't know what was expected of him, but he too grabbed his rifle and beat a hasty retreat into the forest.

From behind the tanks soldiers suddenly sprouted out of the ground and stormed the camp, their guns stuttering and smoking. A jet swept low over the trucks, dropping sacks of white powder that burst like snowballs. Then jeeps came rolling in from the main path.

"Your headquarters have been taken!" an officer shouted gleefully. "Surrender or die!"

* * * *

I wouldn't be so presumptuous as to say I was responsible for losing that war; such claims to glory do not suit my nature. On the front our troops had already surrendered. This final defeat was a mere mopping-up operation, but I suppose it was a humiliating end of our boot camp.

The last few days were devoted to cleaning and returning equipment, then came the farewell celebration. By now discipline had deteriorated. Weeks of tension had broken into a heady feeling. The corporals were practically buddies. Even Gérard had given in, and put up good-naturedly with teasing. The officers too joined in with some kidding, though always crisply; and to all this the commander turned a blind eye.

It was interesting to observe how the 'boys' had turned into 'men'. They were tougher and could endure humiliation. They had learned to live together and co-operate, even if it was just to save their own necks, and they followed orders, otherwise they were the same vulgar, silly boys, armed now, lethal – potential killers.

In some cases there was progress on another level. Philip could tie his gaiters and put on his cartridge-belts at the drop of a hat. And

Hebeli could even feebly defend himself, though this was his downfall.

On the last evening during the height of the revelry, Hebeli actually returned the swift kick a drunken Morin had planted in his bottom. We all cheered and held Morin back, but later he returned with a few buddies. They stripped poor Hebeli of his clothes, hoisted him high in the air, and paraded him yelling and struggling throughout the barracks. We tried to save him but were outnumbered.

I don't know what effect this had on his later life, nor how the others developed. Usually soldiers see each other again in the repetition courses. But since I had been suffering from a minor ailment all of my life, I was advised to get a medical dispensation. When my case came up before an army board, I said I was willing to serve, but my hay fever only permitted me to be a soldier in the winter. The amused and slightly flattered smiles of the officers were followed by a large bold rubber stamp pounded in my 'Little Book of Service': *DIENSTUNTAUGLICH*. I am officially not fit for military service. But when I turn to the section *taxe militaire*, three pages are scrawled full of dates and signatures. In Switzerland not doing your service costs its price. Depending on your income, this can be quite high.

* * * *

Afternoon. It has stopped raining but the sky is still bloated with clouds. Flies bat irascibly at my head. On the way to the station I pass a field of cows placidly cropping the grass, their tails swishing. At my approach they raise their heads, stare wide-eyed and dumb, jaws swinging. Then the station. The small green BAM train is pulling in, clacking to a halt. An old woman with a basket gets on, then a mother and child. Inside I see the reflection of a soldier sitting in the middle window seat. I too board the train, taking the seat next to the door. I open the window and watch the conductor rush into the station house. He comes back lugging a mail bag. The train jolts and slides away. The mother points to some farmhouses, talking to the child, raising its hand to the window. The soldier turns to look and then I see his face. The smooth outlines of his features, the thickish lips, horn-rimmed glasses that do not suit his face, hair cut too short, making his ears stand out and his nose more prominent, more fleshy. He sees me and smiles.

"On leave for the weekend?" I ask.

He nods.

I stand up and walk over to him.

"Do you mind if I sit here?" I ask. "I was once a soldier."

"I know."

I sit down opposite him and look out at ripening fields of wheat floating by on a green sea.

"You've been watching me, haven't you?" he suddenly asks.

"Yes."

"I felt it."

"I hope it hasn't bothered you," I say.

"Well, it's one-sided, isn't it?"

"I don't understand..."

"Of course you do." He grins in an assured way. "I cannot watch you. I can only wonder about you, make guesses and hope. But you know everything about me. You sit back comfortably and watch me any time you please from your...your secure window in the future." He pauses thoughtfully, then adds: "I hate you, Robert."

"You...hate me..."

"Yes, I hate you for your superiority."

We remain silent for a moment. The child points to some sheep on a hill and cries out: *Tu vois, Maman, des moutons!*

"You're mistaken..." I try to make him understand, "I'm not what you think..."

He leans forward and squints in that way he used to when struggling to cope with an unknown situation.

"You mean your dreams haven't come true?"

"My dreams," I laugh. "You have no idea how many burdens you've left me with your...OUR dreams."

"That sounds like defeatism," he sneers.

"No," I hesitate. "You cannot know..."

"Do you want to say that I'm too young? Isn't that what you future people always say about your past selves?"

"No...everything is so unlived," I retort. "Your dreams have not been cast adrift. They are anchored..."

He laughs at this statement, leans back and laughs.

"You've grown fat," he suddenly says. "And that beard! What woman talked you into that?" Then he leans forward again and looks straight into my eyes. "Are you happy?"

How can I answer such a simple question? Only he could ask that.

"I'm not alone," I finally answer. "There is someone waiting. But please, don't ask any more questions."

"Then you are not as superior as I thought," he says, turning to the window.

We are approaching the castle. Its massive towers squat on the hill. Terraced vineyards sweep down from the base of the walls, run over the slopes, and then as the train turns, I catch a glimpse of the lake, swirling in mist, then those ugly suburb blocks ram into position. The train inclines steeply downwards and we coast into Morges.

"I must get out now," I say.

He remains seated, a reflection in the window.

"Stop watching me," he says after a moment. "Leave me in my past world. Perhaps it's better than yours."

I want to argue with him, to shout that it is not yet lived, that his dreams are impossible. He refuses to look at me. Yes, he was always that way, so unreasonable, so obstinate. Nobody could ever say a word to him. For a brief moment I almost admire him, and then I remember I have to hurry.

Someone is waiting.

Roger Bonner today.

A Train of Serious Events

by George Blythe

During the fifties I left Canada for a look around Europe. The first port of call was Paris. A few dollars went a long way and I planned to spend a few days in Marseilles, drift eastwards along the Côte d'Azur and finally travel through northern Italy to Vienna.

I took the first southbound train from Gare de Lyon. It was a bad one, stopping at every station. There were no refreshments and the day became warmer and warmer. Then at Dijon a sleepy voice announced over a loudspeaker that there would be a stop of ten minutes. This would give me ample time to jump off and buy a beer and a bite at a platform stall. But just as I was paying, the train started to move off and I leapt into the nearest compartment, which was nearer the engine than where my baggage was, but it didn't seem to matter since there was a communicating corridor.

After lurching rearwards through a few coaches, I came to a disconcerting halt. It was the tail end of the train and the other half – with my baggage – was disappearing in the other direction.

I got off at the next station, which was rather sleepier and smaller than the last and made my way to the *chef de gare*. He was a slight, amiable man in an office that reeked of stale tobacco and burgundy.

On being told of my plight, he leaned back in his creaky chair and sighed, *"Ah oui! Ça arrive tous les jours."* He was not only philosophical but practical. Reaching for the phone he put in a call to Vallorbe, Switzerland, where the baggage would be impounded by customs. It took an age to come through, the line was bad, and despite the common language he seemed to be having difficulty in describing to his Swiss colleague one of the items, namely the rucksack.

"...et un sac à dos," the *chef de gare* was saying.

"Quelle couleur?" came the precise question from Switzerland.

"Khaki," replied the Frenchman.

"Caca? Comprends pas!" exclaimed the Swiss.

"Non, Non," moaned the man at my end, *"khaki...alors, BRUN!"*

It was an enchanting thought that someone somewhere in a corner of the mountains was blissfully ignorant of our drab, wartime colour. But one thing became clear: I must retrieve my belongings personally since they would cross a frontier unaccompanied, unregistered, and illegally (though a passport was in the rucksack). Another difficulty was that the next train was not due to arrive in Vallorbe till about midnight.

Arrival of the Paris-Milan express in Vallorbe in the old days

On arrival in Switzerland there was a reception committee of three customs officials waiting for me, one of them wearing a kepi. The baggage was on the table in glorious isolation. After brief formalities, I thanked the committee for finding my belongings and apologized for putting them to so much trouble. This earned me a cursory salute from the kepi, who then said that as it was so late they had reserved a hotel room but since they were unaware of my financial means, "it would be rather modest."

Flabbergasted, I could not help saying that never before had I met with such concern by customs officials for a complete stranger, a mere *inconnu*.

This time the man with the kepi gave a snappier, more triumphant salute and said, *"Monsieur, vous étes dans un pays sérieux!"*

My first sight on awakening from a deep slumber in the modest hotel was quite a surprise. The window framed a view of craggy mountains with wreaths of mist swirling slowly down their peaks. The distant sound of cowbells rubbed in the impression of being somewhere else than planned. The change of air after Paris may have also contributed to the augury which led me to accept an accidental detour. I had to see more of this *pays sérieux*.

THE STEREOTYPE CRUNCHER

by Ramón Aguirre

I think anyone living in a foreign country would get an uncomfortable feeling if he discovered that his own experience didn't square with the stereotypes about it. Of course, stereotypes have a limited objective validity, but on the subjective level they serve as indicators; they constitute a set of vaguely valid ideas that help you know what to expect and how to act and react. All the foreigners who have been in a country longer (some not longer) than you have, volunteer invaluable and accurate information about the way people are there. These bits of information may at first be disparate, but a certain number of ideas recur with such frequency that they seem to gel into a kind of unofficial official guide. As one goes through each day or is confronted with a given situation, these notions inevitably come to mind like the echo voice in an old-fashioned movie.

I hear the voice, let's call it ("..."), but what it says never corresponds to what I experience. ("They're very punctual.") Well, for starters, if I had a dollar for every minute I've waited for tardy Swiss friends, I'd have enough money to buy a ranch out West – make that ten dollars.

But even more significant than the experiences with friends are the experiences with people you don't know, total strangers whom you should be able to rely upon not to make any adjustments and just to be themselves. If they don't act the way they're supposed to, who's going to take up the statistical slack?

One thing people always mention is this business of the over-importance of money here. ("Just look around you if you need any convincing. Have you ever seen so many financial institutions? Everybody's either a banker or bookkeeper. Just listen to an average conversation, how many times does money come up and in how many ways? You come from a money-oriented country. Can anything you've ever seen or heard there compete with it?")

I'm not saying I've ever seen anybody over here throw money away but this supposed importance given to money and especially the idea that money is more important than people or human sentiments is simply an exaggeration. Two examples of the opposite come to mind.

I finally managed to get a date with that special girl I couldn't get off my mind. I hadn't been in Switzerland long, and not wanting to make any cultural blunders, I asked my Swiss friends about the ground rules. "Take her to an expensive restaurant; that will make a

Paradeplatz in Zurich is renowned for being the center of Swiss banking. Hardly a place where you would expect to find an alpine musician earning a few centimes here with a 'redesigned' alphorn! Photo D. Dicks.

good impression" was the main item of advice that was given to me. The big night arrived and everything was going perfectly. A light and yet promisingly substantial conversation. Excellent dinner – everything à la carte. I expected my date to order from the left side of the menu, but in view of the fact that what she ordered was so inexpensive, she must have been ordering from the right side. Mindful of the price-impression equation, I thought I'd better make up for this so as not to lose face and, without even trying, I soon had the bill up to over a hundred francs.

Over a hundred francs – in the excitement of getting ready for this important date I had forgotten my wallet. Of course, I didn't notice this until towards the end of the dinner when I started thinking about the bill. ("Don't get out of line, and above all, always be able to pay, and you'll never have any trouble here.") As I involuntarily and inconspicuously went about checking all my pockets for my wallet, I noticed that the waiter noticed. ("They are very distrustful.") But there was no trace of suspicion in his look. One more furtive search of my pockets at least brought in my automatic banking card, but the prospect of leaving my charming, blond-haired, blue-eyed date, hunting about for an automatic bank teller, and making a less than spectacular re-entrance destroyed the momentary consolation.

Well, I took as long as I could to finish my coffee, but how far can you stretch an espresso? By now it was obvious that the waiter knew I didn't have any money. It was also obvious that my heroic attempts to make a good impression would have otherwise made the beginnings of a very romantic evening. "That's it!" I desperately said to myself. "The waiter must have also noticed the total situation. Maybe I could catch him just inside the kitchen door and work something out." Then I heard that voice again. ("They are not a romantic people.") I sadly came to the conclusion that not being romantic automatically excludes romantic empathy. I decided to call the waiter, say with as much grace as possible that I didn't have any hard cash on me, and let fate take its course. As he stood next to me, all I could say was "I..."

Before I could start properly squirming, a broad smile came across his face. "Did you forget your wallet?"

"Yes, I..."

Before I could articulate any facsimile of an explanation he put his smile into words. "That's all right; you can pay me next time."

You're probably thinking he somehow knew I would come back and was sure he would get his money and a permanent customer to boot. Well let me give you another case in point which admits of no such businessman-customer explanation.

Everyone has had a busy day on which he forgets important details. Sometimes it doesn't matter, and sometimes an overlooked detail can upset everything. On one of these days I was so busy concentrating on a myriad of things I had to do that I simply jumped on the streetcar without buying a ticket. No sooner had the doors closed than I realized this. No sooner had I realized this than the inspector came by. ("Don't forget to buy a ticket before getting on a tram or a bus. Getting a fine here for not having a ticket isn't a perfunctory formality. It's an axe of reproval coming down on your head. Everybody else in the streetcar turns toward you with disapproving looks and a slight serves-him-right nod to their neighbors. Some people even openly gloat at you as if to say, 'Good, they finally caught you.' It's a not very minor version of a public execution. Don't laugh. This is very serious. I know a venerable 96-year-old grandmother who would be a totally respected member of her community if she hadn't got a fine for not having a valid ticket in the winter of 1967.")

I'm a firm believer in the honor system, and I had every intention of getting off at the next stop to buy a ticket. But how do you explain to a person whose sole function it is to fine offenders that you're the victim of an attention lapse? Again, the voice: ("These guys do everything BY THE BOOK. Don't even try giving explanations or making excuses if you ever do anything wrong.") The inspector didn't fit this picture at all. He'd noticed my nervousness, as evidenced by my pressing the panic button, and that I was upset with myself. I could see that he really didn't want to give me a fine and he only needed some reasonable explanation. "Honesty is the best policy" I said to myself, and decided to tell him the unembellished truth.

"I'm terribly sorry. I simply forgot to get a ticket. It's the first time that's ever happened."

He had the explanation he needed. "Well, if it's the first time, I'll let you off with a warning, but don't let it happen again." And then, to cap it off, a slight backward tilt of the head, a big smile and a hearty "Have a nice day."

But what convinced me that all these generalizations were sheer nonsense was an experience I had with the stereotype cruncher – a person who utterly destroys entire series of misconceptions: ("They keep everything bottled up inside themselves." "They don't get other people involved." "They don't reach out to other people." "They don't rebel." "They don't go in for nuances." "They don't suffer and even if they do suffer no artistic expression results from it.")

It's the end of the work day at the Bahnhofquai streetcar stop. You can see the load of insufferable bosses, routine work, and griping colleagues weighing down on people's shoulders. Everybody has his/her 'don't-bother-me/leave-me-alone' face on. Everyone has only one desire: to get on that streetcar and get home as quickly as possible. You can cut the tension with a knife. Nobody's going to queue up to get in, they're all going to crowd around the door and make the departing passengers fight to get out. No chance for Miss Lovely to make a graceful exit – no matter what she's wearing, no matter how many curves she has. It's a straight line out for her, too, with nobody stepping back to make room for her or send admiring glances. These people mean business. They want their paid-with-their-taxes/no-nonsense ride out of here, and they want it now.

Can anybody deal with this? Yes: the stereotype cruncher.

There he is ready to step – ride – on stage. He's the streetcar driver. He makes his entrance from the Bahnhofstrasse – a street with an unimaginative name but very imaginative prices. Of course, everybody at the Bahnhofquai stop has noticed him, i.e., the streetcar, at once, but they play it cool and act as if they haven't seen anything or as if it's a matter of course. They know that – like the atomic shock wave – it's going to take him sixty seconds to arrive in front of them. And he knows they know. But he also knows they're bluffing. The Bahnhofquai stop is long enough for two streetcars to stop at the same time, one behind the other: in human terms, one hundred paces, which is a long walk even if you're not carrying anything. In the rush hour you can MISS YOUR STREETCAR if you're not at the right place at the right time.

Coming out of the Bahnhofstrasse our friend makes an elegant right turn onto the Bahnhofplatz and then perches there before making an equally elegant left turn toward the Bahnhofquai stop. At this point he can no longer be ignored and everybody on the platform imperceptibly leans toward him. But he waits until the far section of the stop is occupied by another street car. Now he's got everybody right where he wants them. They have to keep their eye on both streetcars. If the front streetcar leaves before he gets there, they have to be all the way at the end or else our friend will load up and depart before they get on. If the car at the end of the stop doesn't get loaded and leave quickly, our friend will load at the beginning of the stop and depart simultaneously with the leading tram.

The king on his moving metal throne has perched on the Bahnhofplatz stretching the sixty seconds into a psychological eternity. At the first movement of the vehicle, people straighten up like so many human iron filings stirred by the magnetism of the streetcar. As it comes into the first section of the stop, the driver sets such a slow pace that everyone is convinced that the vehicle has to stop at any second. The ones in the middle of the long stop and the ones at the far end even start walking toward him. By the time he's in the first section, all the would-be riders are next to the streetcar waiting for him to stop and open the doors. But he doesn't stop; he just keeps moving at a molasses-in-January pace.

Now the buttons for opening the doors are going by so slowly that everyone can walk along side and take a stab at them, each in his own way: secretaries, at this time of day unmindful of the ten-finger-system and trying to push the button with the wrong digit but still with the typewriter touch; shy people, now aggressively trying to spear the thing with their index fingers; die-hard optimists slapping at the button with splayed fingers in the hope that something will hit it; people for whom this is the final frustration of the day and who are content to slam any part of the streetcar with the heel of their fists in the general area of the button. People who don't have that much physical energy left, limit themselves to emitting oaths.

In short, everybody has come out of his/her shell; everybody is involved; everybody is expressing himself/herself; they're all together. The driver has succeeded where countless itinerant sing-along-with-me musicians have failed. Granted, as they trudge along side the tram, they are mainly united in hating the driver, but there's more to it than that. Deep, deep down inside they are also unconsciously taking stock; they are somehow vaguely aware that the driver's been going around in circles for hours, that there's a little bit more between them than a correctly punched ticket. On the outside however, feelings are running high. The driver has a potential lynch-mob on his hands, as anger increases in geometrical progression to every additional step that has to be taken. No one is even trying to push the button now, they're all just lumbering along and staring daggers at the driver who has brought things so dangerously near the exploding point that there doesn't seem to be any graceful way out of this.

In the meantime the streetcar at the far end of the stop ahead of him has left: the driver still has fifty passenger steps to work with. This gives him enough room to speed up suddenly and simulate driving away for about thirty steps. A combination of surprise, shock and disbelief freezes everybody dead in their tracks. THERE'S NOW NO RIDE OUT. Before they can even start trying to come to terms with this situation, the driver stops the tram at the far end and invitingly opens the doors. The psychological blow he has just dealt the would-be passengers has not only drained them of all their aggression toward him, it's drained them of all their aggression, period.

They all get onto the streetcar, having gone through a cathartic experience. On the outside, faces are a little less stony, so I conclude that inside hearts are a little lighter. Nobody is going up to the driver to complain.

Rebel, artist, mass healer, comedian, practical joker, psychological philanthropist, choreographer, dramatist, actor, philosopher – this man doesn't fit into any of the standard 'national' character categories. And he's much more than just 'out of character'. He's a stereotype cruncher.

Everybody keeps telling me that my experiences are the exception, and that the proverbial exception confirms the proverbial rule. Perhaps, but at the present rate, in order for everything to balance out, I'll have to live in Switzerland another hundred years.

LIFE ON THE FRINGE

by Trevor Watts

Straight as Tell's arrow, Rietmühlestrasse stretched away between the flat maize fields. The blue-clad farmer moved his battered little mowing machine over to the side so that our bicycles could pass. My Tasmanian friend, enjoying his second overseas holiday in eighteen months, gave a gasp of astonishment. "Why, it's just like China," he exclaimed.

That had certainly not been my reaction on walking around this village in the St. Gall Rhine Valley on that first evening almost twenty years earlier. True, there were the homely farm smells, but they evoked vivid memories of a Nottinghamshire childhood.

This article is about life in a part of Switzerland away from the big cities, but away from the well-beaten tourist tracks as well. It is about a society which, during the last two decades, has traded-in part of its rural innocence in exchange for increased material prosperity, but which has not yet had to pay too high a price in terms of environmental deterioration. In other words, it is about the everyday nitty-gritty of a semi-rural area.

So – what was it like in 1968, and what is it like now? In the late sixties this village, which numbered perhaps four thousand inhabitants, was a fairly thriving, self-contained farming community with most of the virtues and failings of a closely-knit, little-travelled society. The movements of newcomers were followed closely and with great interest. When sitting in a local restaurant over a beer a week or two after arriving, I was more than mildly surprised to be asked by the waitress whether it wasn't perhaps uncomfortable to sleep on that bed with the springs coming through the mattress. Further enquiries revealed that she was the daughter of the kindly *Putzfrau* who tidied up my bedsitter each day.

I was tempted here by the offer of a job in light industry. One of the attractions of living in Switzerland is that nearly every village in the valleys or in the lower foothills has a large number and variety of businesses, in addition to the odd factory or two, so there is no need for young local people to seek work elsewhere unless that is what they want. Accelerating industrialisation in the countryside has however led to greater openness and increased mobility, so that today the person who has never travelled is regarded as the oddity, and there is a much greater readiness to accept strangers.

Nevertheless, newcomers often seriously underrate the difficulties of living in this sort of environment. To begin with, there is the language problem. Country people in Eastern Switzerland do not in general relish speaking High German, so it is worth persevering with attempts to both understand and speak the local dialect. Then there is the slow learning process involved in comprehending all of those slight cultural differences and thought patterns. Here is a crumb of consolation: Many of the German-speaking Swiss from the big cities have difficulty in acclimatising to life here, and the French-speaking Swiss often have problems similar to those of the English-speaking community!

In general, men of English mother tongue tend to settle better than their non-working wives, who may feel isolated; there is, however, some evidence that women who had a boarding-school education can cope better than those who have led a more sheltered existence.

In any event, it does take a long time to become involved in local social life. Whether this is important to the person concerned depends on individual temperament. There are very many cultural activities going on here, even if at a somewhat parochial level, and almost every type of sports facility is available.

Off the beaten track on a bike, discovering the countryside.
Photo by SNTO.

The first rule for settling into these surroundings is: Greet people, whether you know them or not. After a time you will be recognised and greeted by name (your surname, if an unusual one by local standards, may come to mind fairly easily). The problem is to remember what the other party is called, although there is a fair chance that it will be one of the three or four surnames which account for most of the village population. This is where a bicycle comes in useful; you can start off with a hearty *"Grüezi, Herrrr..."* and trail off into an indecipherable mumble as you move out of earshot, still racking your brains. (This custom of greeting strangers may cause you problems when you return to your own country, where the suspicious but unspoken reaction may be: "What does he/she want?")

The second rule is to accept the homely blunt earthiness of the locals. They are kindly, honest people, and if you lost anything you will almost certainly get it back. Bicycles may disappear if they are left unlocked (there is the odd delinquent youngster anywhere), but the crime rate generally is very low. Children are safe from practically everything except for mad motorists, and can otherwise be left to wander around freely alone. There is however an outside chance that your cat, if sufficiently large and succulent, may end up in someone's cooking pot. (Whether locals or foreigners are responsible for this one is hotly disputed.)

If you have children, you may well wonder what the local educational system is like. We were initially somewhat apprehensive; our fears proved to be totally unfounded. There are few disciplinary problems and the schooling in this particular area, at any rate, is second to none – although admittedly we are fortunate in that the local "Kantonsschule" (sixth-form college) is right on the doorstep.

For the newcomer there is the question of where to live. Clearly, rented accommodation here is substantially cheaper than in the big cities. Property was at one time kept very closely within the family and passed on by inheritance, but the building booms of the Seventies and early Eighties have created many opportunities for foreigners holding permanent residence permits to buy apartments or, more interestingly, new houses. The rate of owner- occupation is probably well over the Swiss average of about 30%. Once bought, property is rarely sold again in a hurry by the locals and the reaction to the news that a foreigner is taking the plunge is: "So you've decided to settle here?"

Life on the flat north-eastern fringe of Switzerland can be very satisfying. It is however not something for the committed city-dweller, and this is where the experiences of that far-off rural Nottinghamshire childhood have proved to be a great advantage.

Trevor Watts.

On Being an Outsider

by Jane Christ

One of the pleasures of middle age, I am finding out, is the fun of discovering the common threads in the fabric of one's life. These are the threads of continuity which have remained throughout the various pattern changes, role changes, geographic changes and age changes that a given life is subject to. When a person is younger, the attention is drawn to all the possibilities that lie ahead and to the fun of imagining what it would be like to be like this or to live in that place. This forward looking approach continues to a certain extent throughout life. But somewhere along the way, there comes the realization that life is different from what one had imagined it would be and that part of this difference has to do with who one is or rather who one has become.

It is important for me to describe the retrospective spirit in which I write this, as I otherwise might sound like someone describing a self-fulfilled prophecy in which she first saw herself "as an outsider" and then sought out life experiences which would confirm this. Quite to the contrary, before coming to Switzerland, I had never seen myself as such an experienced outsider. Because there has been nothing quite so striking in all my life as the experience of being an outsider in Switzerland, I have been forced to come to terms with this phenomenon on a very personal level.

In July 1979, as a 42-year-old American clinical social worker, I had left my full-time job and after-hours private practice in psychotherapy to move to the Basle area with my husband of six months, a Swiss-American psychiatrist. Both of us had recently been divorced from our prior spouses and we could bring only two of our seven children with us. For educational and custody reasons we had to leave the others in the United States. As we soon found out, there was much more that we both had left behind: friends, co-workers, the spirit of being part of a team, a spacious house and all the conveniences of life in suburban America.

My husband had family here and a definite job to do. I had neither. Our experiences differed in my being an "outsider". This quality was masked at first by his family's pleasure at having the long-lost son and brother return and by my having the outward trappings of an "insider", a Swiss last name and Swiss citizenship. But as time passed, the euphoria of the arrival subsided and the day to day routine established itself. Because of the different language, I was outside of most conversations that included anyone but my husband and the children. At the German language classes I attended, I was older than everyone else in the class. Not only could I not practice my profession, because of the new language and the lack of contact with English-speaking people, but I also found many other daily routines to be different including having to cook meals with different measurements, different temperature scales and a different vocabulary of ingredients.

After having lived in Switzerland for eight years and having located the American Women's Club and other English-speaking expatriates, I know that many have had a similar outsider- experience at first and have indeed survived, and overcome. Depending on their age on arrival, their talents, their interests and the length of their stay, many have forged their own style of healthy adaptation.

In addition to those who have eventually done well and settled into Swiss life without problems, there were other newcomers who had to overcome a great many problems both in their employment and in their family life. They complained a great deal at first but later found a way to accommodate to the new kind of life with its difficulties.

A third group of people who at first seemed quite different from the other two groups came to my attention as a clinician and therapist. Surprisingly enough, despite their being no longer recognizable as outsiders, they were expressing acute dissatisfaction with their life in Switzerland and suffering extraordinary emotional pain with severe psychological symptoms. In their initial adjustment to Switzerland they had distanced themselves from the English-speaking community and had completely embraced the language and customs of the native Swiss. It is not surprising that their sudden change of heart toward negativism in regard to Switzerland had shocked and confused their Swiss families and friends, accompanied as it was by depressive and paranoid-appearing ideas. Help then was sought from an English speaking therapist as someone who was perceived as standing outside of the hated system.

At first I was not sure how to interpret the problems of this third group of people. Were cultural differences at the heart of the matter or only a contributing factor? I have since come to the conclusion that this third group of people had adapted too fast to the new culture. They did not sufficiently appreciate their status as outsiders, but tried to "get in" as quickly as possible, therewith doing harm to their own individuality and their self-esteem.

I have come to appreciate the special delicacy of the outsider's status, or shall we say the paradoxical quality of that status. It is a status which is rarely sought after. It can be tolerated and even enjoyed, but only when it is partial and understood. Like a scab on a wound, it should not be removed too eagerly or hastily, and it is best left to fall off, unnoticed, when the new skin of personal identity has formed underneath.

In my life, I have had quite a bit of experience as an outsider in the United States which, no doubt, has indirectly influenced my present experience. I was an only child in a family which consisted of four adults. I therefore know well and dislike the feeling of being discounted and unable to participate in some activities. I was a Protestant growing up in a predominantly Jewish neighborhood with a scattering of Roman Catholics. From this experience, I have carried with me the frustration of knowing that vague, even translucent barriers can still powerfully limit the scope of relationships. My family was Republican and the neighborhood belonged primarily to the Democratic Party. In the intensity of war-time America, political differences such as these were escalated to treason and could not be discussed openly. Then, coming from a lower middle-income family, I dared to attend a high-ranking, elite women's college in search of a better education. There the students came mostly from the upper, business and professional classes and I had not counted on the effect of feelings of social inferiority. After that, career moves meant I could also have the experience of being a transplanted Easterner in two different sections of the United States: the Midwest and the South. Both of these areas tend to view Easterners with skepticism and defensive discounting; Easterners are expected to be arrogant and exploitive. Upon marriage to my second husband, six months before moving to Europe, I had the additional experience of becoming a stepparent. As modern sociologists and psychologists have found out, the status of a stepparent is, above all else, the status of an outsider in a pre-formed family unit. Fortunately for me, this aspect of my experience was perhaps ameliorated by the move to Switzerland and by the fact that it was shared by my husband. Also, by that time most of our children were teenagers or young adults.

Being an outsider can broaden the mind more than mere travel can ever do and it can sensitize one to the many subtle ways culture defines and prescribes in our lives and in the lives of others. Depending on the kind of person we are, we each find some things easier to change and accommodate to than others. For me, language has been the hardest as it seems to lie closest to the core of my self. But this I was able to turn into an advantage by becoming an English teacher. Whatever I have lost in opportunity for clinical practice, I have gained many times over through teaching English as a foreign language. It has served as a vehicle for learning about many new and interesting facets of my mother-tongue and it has given me a way to make meaningful contacts with Europeans – Swiss, French, Germans and Yugoslavians. Being perceived as an outsider has helped me build rapport with my students. They seem to have had less of a need to feel defensive about making mistakes with someone who is even less fluent in their language.

In response to my first point about the outsider's status being rarely sought, some may say that there are always some people who do try to be, or at least to appear, different. However, when we look more closely at these people, we see that they are aiming to appear better than the rest and are not simply standing outside the mainstream. "Outsider" is more of a descriptive term from the point of view of inside some reference group.

If one has acquired the label "outsider", then, it behooves him to investigate its benefits and not to embrace the culture of the mainstream blindly. In any case it seems wiser to become more of a participant observer at first, noting similarities and differences and at the same time continuing relationships to fellow expatriates. This is the way most immigrant populations successfully rooted themselves in the New World. They first lived in ghettos or neighborhoods of people from the old country and only gradually permitted themselves to melt into the mainstream, usually enriching it with their own customs and traditions. Here in Switzerland a different approach to outsiders has been used which benefits neither the outsider nor the Swiss. Outsider groups are dispersed and not encouraged to settle in neighborhoods. Their need for affiliation, support and the validation of their own culture is thus thwarted and denied.

Until recently, foreign women who married Swiss men (as in my case) automatically became Swiss. This special concession to foreign women was due, no doubt, to the belief that women were weak, pliable and derived their identity from their husbands. Foreign men were seen differently. The new law, designed to equalize the rights for men and women, is much more reasonable as it allows for an adaptation period and it requires that the request for insider status come from the individual person.

Why is it that outsiders in Switzerland, whatever their social standing or category, are prone to feel of so little worth even after having joined the mainstream and learned the local dialect? It has been claimed in certain Basle families that even Swiss people born in Zurich are seen as outsiders, though they have lived most of their lives in Basle. It has been difficult for me to take such attitudes seriously and in fact my first reaction was one of disbelief.

Coming from the United States, which is a nation of former outsiders, I can see why I had trouble understanding this aspect of Swiss culture. To be an outsider in the United States, however much it results in a temporary disequilibrium and social handicap, is a much more benign condition, perhaps because it is so temporary and easily modifiable. In the United States the responsibility for change and adjustment is left more to the individual and more importance is attached to what one does than who one is by birth or origin.

Because Switzerland seems to be more of a group-oriented society which places great importance on the ascribed status provided by family membership and place of origin, it can be expected to offer the outsider a different system of cultural rewards and punishments than that which exists in the United States. In Switzerland individual differences and responsibilities receive less recognition; conformity is greatly emphasized and change of status is seen as not particularly desirable nor easily achievable.

Similarities in the economic and political system of countries can be deceptive and do not imply there is an underlying social and cultural similarity. When we take these underlying cultural differences into consideration we can more accurately see the puzzling cross currents in which an outsider in Switzerland can get caught. He is urged to adapt and conform to the ways of the majority because this is a group-oriented society. At the same time, the rewards for this adaptation are withheld because the factors which make him an outsider are beyond his control and immutable, deriving as they do from his family background and place of origin.

In the Swiss-German-speaking part of Switzerland, one of the important by-products of the dialect is that it provides a quick indication of the regional origins of the speaker, thereby revealing whether one is an insider or an outsider. It seems that one cannot really understand the importance attached to the various regional dialects — especially in view of the practical barriers they create vis-a-vis the French-speaking Swiss and the neighboring Germans — unless one understands the Swiss preoccupation with group identity and the significance of one's place of origin.

What have I learned thus far from my own cumulative experiences as an outsider and my observation of other outsiders? First, on the cultural level, beware of apparent similarities! It is a mistake to be in too great a hurry to change one's outsider status before one has had a chance to develop a real understanding and feeling for the new culture. There can be real psychological repercussions if one is too quick to change. Once the former ways of feeling and living are abruptly split off from consciousness and submerged in the unconscious, they can reappear in an unpleasant form, perhaps as a severe psychological problem or a physical illness. This was the fate of the "over-adapters" mentioned earlier. Their precocious adaptation amounted to self-devaluation and self-negation.

It appears to be an insufficiently publicized fact that much can be learned from the vantage point of an outsider. Such a person will be privy to all sorts of information and confidences that are denied to the insider because of his perceived power. The outsider's perceived weakness can thus become his strength. There are also some additional compensations. Because he is not expected to know and therefore not obligated to be bound by all the local traditions, his participation is on a voluntary basis and he is freer.

The second principle I have learned is *vive la difference!* Each person seems to have to work out his own particular solution to the outsider status. One's own personal style, previous life experience and family provenience will all play a role. There is no one perfect way and those who hold up the rosy-colored recollections of their own adaptational process as universally applicable to all, do more harm than good. There is no one solution that will fit everyone. Each successful adaptation needs an individual healthy integration of a previous sense of self into the demands of the new environment. A healthy adaptation, like many other forms of healthy change and growth, develops best when it comes in response to a gradually felt inner pressure to grow and expand the self and not out of a need to obtain the instant gratification of dependency by submerging one's own identity in favor of identifying with the insiders. For such a healthy adaptation to occur, sufficient time, patience and good will are needed.

At this point, after eight years in Switzerland, I am quite comfortable with my outsider status and as I have become more comfortable, I have felt more accepted in general. The possibility of returning to the United States to live, at least in the near future, no longer seems as attractive as it once was. I feel myself to be in a rather stable middle position between two cultures, able to enjoy them both and reluctant to choose between them.

Jane Christ. Photo C. Roessiger.

Hymn to Switzerland

by Homer D. Wheaton

Oh! You, my Switzerland,
Always the country for me.
You hold my heart and soul.
God save you eternally.

Photo SNTO.

O Du, mein Schweizerland

Music by Homer D. Wheaton
Words by Eliot B. Wheaton

O Du, mein Schwei-zer-land, bist stets das Land für mich. Dir bleibt mein Herz und See-le treu, Gott schütz' Dich e-wig-lich.

Getting Acquainted with Swiss Food

by May Zimmerli-Ning

Swiss food does not have the connotation nor the reputation of being anything special as far as I am aware. One never seems to hear of Swiss food outside of Switzerland!

My first contact with Swiss food of any kind was an exhilarating experience which has stayed vividly in my mind for twenty-five years. I was a student in England then who was used to British institutional food the quality of which I leave to your imagination. On a hot summer day at the main railway station in Zurich we had arrived too early to meet our Swiss friend. My companion and I decided to venture to the station restaurant on the terrace. Having no knowledge of German, we searched down the menu for signs of recognition. Alas, we found something that read like ice cream with rum. What a great idea – a bit of the Caribbean here in Zurich! When the order came, it was a huge tall basin blanketed in a mountain of whipped cream! I learned then that *Rahm* does not mean rum. It was anyhow rather strange to me then, ice cream with cream!

My contact with home cooking began first, of course, with cheese fondue. My Swiss friends warned me with all good intentions: you must first rub the inside of your fondue pot thoroughly with pressed fresh garlic, don't forget to grate the cheese yourself and use the right proportions, the wine must first be warmed up before putting the freshly grated cheese in, the cheese must be stirred into the wine slowly in small portions. I did all as instructed, and the final slimy product was one thick rubbery mass swimming in an opaque liquid. Any attempt at securing a forkful of this was rewarded with an inseparable string of cheese traversing the whole table on its way to one's mouth!

Today I can make a terrific fondue. I do not follow any instructions, and throw in all the cheese together – any sorts of cheese which I happen to have on hand – in one big splash, and stir in everything. It all turns out fine!

Another cheese dish which the Swiss are very fond of eating, especially in winter, is *Raclette*. This consists of melted cheese which has either been cut from a large round block of cheese beforehand or scraped off the block after it has been heated below a hot grill. Inevitably there are always bits of cheese that get burned and the odor produced is not appreciated by all! *Raclette* is eaten with boiled potatoes in their skins. Nowadays, many *Raclette* lovers melt their

May Zimmerli-Ning with her daughters, Franziska on the left and Christine on the right, enjoying a cheese Fondue with a Chinese touch. Photo R. Zimmerli.

portions of cheese in small square pans used with special spirit burners or electric grills which are placed in the center of the dining table. Each guest prepares his or her own *Raclette*. My brilliant idea was to use this same equipment with other ingredients for frying eggs, sausages and bacon in these tiny pans instead of having burned cheese. Many Swiss and non-Swiss friends think it's great and I get a big kick out of eating **square** eggs!

The Swiss are most partial to sweet foods and often make a meal out of sweet rather than savoury dishes. What I would call breakfast cereal would be a proper evening meal for my husband and subsequently of course, for all the four children. Yes, I am talking about the *Birchermüesli*. This is a kind of health food first invented by Dr. Bircher. It is made up of lots of raw oats, fresh apples cut up in small pieces, nuts, raisins and sugar plus a hefty dose of cream as well as milk. The oats and nuts soak up the milk and presto, you have a mush *(Müesli)* which looks like fancy porridge, only this one is cold.

Because members of my family have a variety of likes and dislikes in taste, I have adapted this popular dish substituting this for that so that besides oats, the *Müesli* I make resembles anything but the original one Dr. Bircher invented! Mind you, my concoction must be quite palatable since Swiss friends have asked me for my recipe.

What I would call a dessert – an open fruit pie or tart called *Waie* here – can also be a complete Swiss meal. Over the past 20 years I've spent many afternoons in our kitchen rolling out pastry and peeling apples, or de-stoning plums or apricots to produce five or six large pizza-sized fruit pies for one meal!

Geschnelzeltes nach Zürcher Art or any other *Art* is fun when it comes to describing the way veal should be cut. One talks of chopped, diced or sliced meat, or meat in strips, all of which are not correct. So I say "pieces of meat" when I explain it to our non-Swiss visitors.

What's more, naming the cuts of meat in Switzerland is a science of its own. Not only are the cuts all different, their names are most extraordinary with a purely regional note to them. When we moved from Berne to Basle in the very early years of my acquaintance with Switzerland, my husband had to accompany me to the butcher as interpreter. Goodness knows, he needed an interpreter himself! In Basle, the loin of pork is known by a name none other than that of my husband's family. Imagine his surprise when we first entered the butcher's shop and heard his name proclaimed loudly and clearly by the butcher to another customer! He hurried forward to acknowledge his pleasure, overwhelmed by the good manners of the Basle people, wondering how on earth the butcher knew his name!

Fondue Bourguinonne is always a sort of gastronomic hazard to me. This dish was originally imported from France. It consists of cooking small cubes of raw beef at the table by securing the meat onto a long metal fork and dipping it in a pot of very hot oil until it is cooked to one's satisfaction much like the way the pieces of bread are dipped in cheese fondue. The cooked meat is removed from the metal fork and dipped in different sauces before eating. This dish has caused some excitement in our house when the oil bubbled over and spluttered into our eyes when our children dipped the meat first in the sauce and **then** into the boiling oil. Or the oil has turned into flames dancing down the side of the little hot copper pot. I've watched in horror as our youngest one was just about to put the hot metal fork straight into her mouth! Ah, but when done properly, what a fine dish!

There is a similar popular dish here called *Fondue Chinoise*. The only difference is that paper-thin strips of beef are dipped in bouillon instead of oil. How much finer it is when the sauces are Chinese! That's the way I've learned to feel at home with Swiss cooking. In fact lots of things about Switzerland get tastier with a bit of soy sauce here, a dab of ginger there, a dash of sesame oil just for fun and presto, one has the best of both worlds!

Changing Gods

by Marcel Bucher

Along the tortuous path we travel through life, the sceneries and the people change as in a kaleidoscope; but the bright colours of the child's fantastic world gradually lose their splendour until the adult person, when looking at the world around, feels like gazing into a clouded mirror. Even the gods may change in our fast-changing world, with foreign deities replacing the local ones, as happened in ancient Rome when the victorious legions brought home the mysterious Egyptian goddess Isis to the seven-hilled city.

I remember enchanted days in rural Appenzell, below the Säntis mountain, where as a boy I spent several months in a children's home at the beginning of World War II. Those were truly arcadian times with roads free of motorcars and the countryside, so it seemed then, still vastly dominated by a genuine herdmen's culture.

Farmer boys often walked around in their colourful Appenzell costumes and amazed us by their earrings, which in those days normally were the exclusive privilege of the fair sex. These exotic creatures were unable to communicate with us by normal human speech, but appeared to sing strange incantations, drawing sounds slowly upward from deep down in the belly until they bubbled forth one by one in a curious yodelling, not resembling any European language but rather the dialect of African tribesmen. At first, we usually did not understand the meaning of their slow-motion yodelling, but always had to ask again what they meant. Invariably, the young "tribesmen" then engaged in long-winded explanations of their cowheards' palaver, accompanied by vivid gestures. The situation was reminiscent of a Negro trying to explain things to a missionary visiting the "dark continent" in the nineteenth century. At that time, almost every valley in the mountainous regions of Switzerland had its separate dialect.

Coming from the lower regions of Zurich, these Appenzell boys did not seem to me to form part of our modern world, but rather appeared as remnants of an old arcadian herdmen's culture, such as the one when the Indian god Krishna walked the earth and danced with the lovely Gopis, the divine maiden herding the sacred cows. Similar to ancient India, the Appenzell meadows and roads then belonged to the cows instead of to tourists and motorcars, the latter of which were immobilized by petrol shortage. Neither ugly apartment buildings in grey concrete nor tasteless clusters of holiday chalets marred the serenely beautiful landscape which resembled one of those naive Appenzell paintings that have in the meantime achieved worldwide fame.

In the evening glow, the majestic Säntis mountain towered like a reddish fortress of Alpine gods above the dark green hues of the lower Kronberg ridge, whose thick woods populated our infantile imagination with fairies, elves and elemental spirits of the most varied kind. Crawling through dense thickets of young fir trees, we sometimes arrived at an enchanted miniature meadow – a dancing ground of elves? Of course, the elves had quickly vanished before our footsteps, but they had left messengers of their magic world behind, weird creatures seemingly immobilized by a spell and dripping with dew: redcaps, chanterelles, boletus as well as numerous other toadstools and fungi, some of them resembling corals sitting on ocean reefs and praying with eerily twisted fingers to a long-forgotten heathen god.

When we looked down steep ravines into deep pools of the river Urnäsch, miniature nymphs seemed to dance ballets around sunbeams piercing the crystal-clear water. Almost every pebble at the bottom stood out distinctly in those unpolluted days. The nymphs, of course, were happy trout which had never experienced the poisoning of their playground by chemicals. Nature appeared to me then as one living being, much as Hinduism traditionally perceives it. And it was a closed, protected world, entirely Swiss, where pagan lore with its imps, trolls, elves, fairies, witches and mountain ghosts supremely ruled the forests and the alps, while only grudgingly leaving the villages proper to the domain of the Christian church.

Of course, this wholly intact world existed merely in our boyish imagination – all around Switzerland, Europe was in flames, with Stuka bombers diving down on defenceless cities to the terrible tune of their screeching sirens, leaving death and devastation behind. But the clamour of war did not reach our peaceful haven in the Appenzell mountains, seemingly protected by benevolent elves and fairies.

The war ended, bringing peace to the outside world and unheard-of prosperity to Switzerland. But the colours of my enchanted boyhood's world grew steadily duller. Grey concrete began to devour childhood's green meadows, burying them under freeways and monotonous tenement buildings. Good roads were built, which enabled even the remotest valleys and villages to be linked to the consumer society in a matter of hours or even minutes. The ephemeral elves and fairies fled the noise of the motor vehicles, which village youngsters now used to drive to well-paid jobs in lowland towns and cities, shedding in the process their strange yodelling dialects so as not to be ridiculed by their city colleagues.

In our childhood days, we city boys had grown up well-acquainted with rural life, as we had to help farmers during those difficult years. We were not estranged from nature as is often the case with today's youth; on the contrary, we lived close to it and formed part of it. But after the great war, we had to submit to the harsh initiation into the unimaginative world of adults. The twitter of birds in hedges at the first golden sunbeams in the morning gave way to the clatter of typewriters in plain offices and the deafening noise of lathes in grimy factory workshops. Nature became a mere matter of weekends. But even so, it withdrew more and more from us together with the arcadian gods of childhood - the imps, witches, fairies, elves and ghosts. During our Sunday walks outside the city, rivers exuded a chemical smell and no merry fishes appeared to dance in their murky waters.

The monotonous office work in Zurich could not provide a substitute for the lost world of dew-dripping forests with fungi resembling fairy-tale creatures, nor the alps with their myriads of lovely flowers. Imposing bank buildings seemed to crush the individual and to preach the power of a cold and hard god: Mammon, to whom only money is sacred. Luckily, Zurich does not only consist of the financial district, but has many quaint and lovely sights to offer, among them lush lakeside parks and ornate Art Nouveau mansions.

Maybe some elemental spirit of childhood's days guided my steps on a gloomy November day toward that esoteric temple of exotic gods and demons known as the Rietberg Museum. It is housed in the imposing Wesendonck mansion of classistic design and encased like a jewel in a park with age-old trees of solemn beauty. Inside, I found again a fantastic world somewhat similar to the one dominating my childhood, but with foreign overtones.

During the war, non-European faces were an extremely rare sight in Switzerland. All refugees came from neighbouring countries. I still remember a thrilling moment at the Bahnhofstrasse, when, as a boy, I discovered such a fabulous creature as was then a real Chinese. I scrutinized his skin closely, feeling considerable disappointment at its light brown colour instead of bright canary yellow as expected. Exotic people and exotic gods were largely absent from my all-Swiss boyhood's world. This changed rapidly after the war, when non-European faces became a common sight in Zurich. In the sixties, even a mythical people like the Tibetans suddenly emerged in flesh and blood, known hitherto only from accounts of hardy explorers. They set up their shrines in the Swiss countryside in order to worship strange-looking deities.

Stepping over the threshold of the Rietberg Museum, however, I did not meet foreign people, discovering instead hall after hall of strange deities and idols probably hating the guts of each other in this forced company, since they belonged to the most diverse cults. A familiar touch was provided at least by the fearsome masks from the Swiss Lötschental, whose uncanny aspect vied with grizzly idols of South-Sea tribes. But on the whole this mute congregation of images came from other continents and past ages.

The Villa Wesendonck in Zurich today accomodates the Rietberg Museum with the collection of non-European art donated to the City of Zurich in 1952 by Baron Eduard von der Heydt. Photo SNTO.

The serene features of a meditating Buddha carried the message that deliverance from suffering is achieved through wisdom: the changing phenomena of the world are just illusionary clouds, obscuring and barring the path to true enlightenment reached by the detached mind.

When I stepped across the threshold into another room, the dispassionate teaching of the enlightened Buddha instantly evaporated in the fiendish glare of gruesome reddish eyes. A master of repulsive art had inserted them into the empty sockets of a human skull wierdly modelled over with clay. It seemed like a South-Sea cannibal's eerie dream come true in a city preferring to nibble exquisite patisserie in elegant cafés. Instead of delicacies, the ghoulish skull rather evoked a gruesome cannibalistic banquet with tam-tam drums beating their hollow rhythm while tattooed savages devour the flesh of slain enemies, watching their shaman evoke fierce battles with wild gesticulations, his shadow dancing behind him like a jungle demon. At least, such was the effect produced on my still imaginative mind. Wood-carved totem poles painted in fleshy colours overwhelmed me with their intricate detail as well as the hideous and obscene imagination of their artistically gifted creators, who seemed to vie with one another as to who was able to achieve absolute masterpieces of repulsive monstrosity.

While outside the windows of this brightly illuminated temple of foreign gods, the mournful dusk shrouded the beautiful park in a deathly grey growing steadily darker, the fiendish grimaces of these cannibalistic idols revelled in dazzling electric light, contrasting vividly with the lifeless November nature. They gave the impression of having truly come to life, grinning in fiendish triumph at me as if rejoicing in having actually driven out the benevolent fairies and elves who had dominated the lost world of my childhood.

Certainly, the Wild Hunt haunting our mountains according to legend during terrible dark *Föhn* nights, when tall trees would break like matches, was awe-inspiring and frightening, as tradition told us these were the resurrected legions of the pagan god Wodan. But at the same time, it was familiar home-grown lore, whereas these sinister, foreign devils came from a world of dark and savage cannibals populated by even darker demons and fetishes.

All around, grotesque and sinister masks and figures grinned and stared in eerie silence at me, some of them strangely gesticulating in their spellbound immobility until I felt like an involuntary participant at a witches' Sabbath and hastily fled this uncanny company. (I seemed to be the sole visitor of the museum.) As my footsteps strangely echoed through the stately museum halls, I passed lovely scrolls showing fantastic Chinese landscapes, alternating with Japanese engravings from which fierce samurais threatened me with drawn swords. Unlike the South-Sea idols, they did not frighten me.

And then I was surrounded by Hindu deities sculptured in bronze, presided over by what appeared to be their master, a four-armed god dancing sublimely inside a wheel of bronze flames. Unlike the idols left behind, his divine Excellency did not grin or grimace at me in a fiendish manner. The face of this magnificent work of art depicting the powerful god Shiva lacked any demonic expression, seeming strangely indifferent, aloof and even insipid. This astonished me all the more after having read the description of the world-famous sculpture: Shiva was shown performing the dance creating the Universe, the end of which he would again celebrate in the dance of destruction. As a complex deity embodying both creation, preservation and destruction, he would go on performing his eternal dance through countless cycles of transient universes, emerging and vanishing like clouds. Triumphantly, Shiva crushed under his dancing feet Muyalaka, the demon of sin and ignorance, although paradoxically he embodied these dark aspects too. Actually, as a sinister god haunting burying sites, he had been offered human sacrifices until comparatively recent times, while other worshippers venerated him precisely for his infinite compassion. Notwithstanding all this, the sculpture of the demonic god did not inspire any fear when I gazed at it. Indeed, his forearms made the sacred Mudra gesture "Have no fear!" Even Shiva's murderous wife Kali, whose bronze kept him company, looked harmless, her garland of human skulls barely recognizable. Various peaceful Hindu gods stood near the presiding Lord of the Dance, as otherwise he would probably have felt lonely in the cold and dark Zurich November and longed all the more for the scorching heat of India. What curious destiny had brought this fantastic deity to the sober and unemotional city of smart and down-to-earth financiers?

The description mentioned the bronze as belonging to the collection of Baron von der Heydt. The name sounded familiar, and I remember that this was the principal initiator of the esoteric community on Monte Verità above Ascona which endeavoured to overcome Western materialism by theosophy, vedanta, yoga and other Eastern philosophies and practices. That such an enlightened man should collect sculptures depicting Oriental deities seemed quite plausible. On the other hand, Monte Verità – the Mountain of Truth – in the sunny Ticino was certainly a more appropriate place for Shiva to perform his cosmic world-preserving dance than business-minded Zurich, a city more likely to venerate Mammon than the fantastic Hindu god. What strange path had Shiva followed from India in order to dazzle staid Zurich burghers by his eternally immobilized dance, so gracious and so free from the sorrows afflicting us ordinary mortals?

While I was pondering these matters, the museum's silence was broken by what seemed halting footsteps, although I was quite sure to be its sole visitor. And unmistakably, the footsteps steadily approached the hall where I stood gazing at Shiva. Had one of the gruesome South-Sea idols suddenly overcome its immobility by sorcerer's magic to pursue me with a fiendish purpose, bloodshot eyes glaring triumphantly? Coming nearer, the uncanny footsteps began to sound more normal until not a ghastly South-Sea idol made its appearance, but an ordinary mortal in flesh and blood with plain features instead of a demoniac grimace: the museum's attendant told me politely that they would close soon.

So I reluctantly left Shiva and the abode of foreign gods, stepping into the dark night. A spectral fog shrouded the stately trees in sepulchral white. As I walked down a steep path, everything seemed colourless and dead except the museum building with its still brightly lit windows. When I looked back, it appeared to me like some haunted castle, where weird foreign gods from all over the world were staging an exotic Walpurgis Night to celebrate their jubilant triumph over nature's mourning under November's gloomy sky. Inside the museum's magic shelter Shiva continuously defeated death in his eternal dance of creation. The contrast between this living god and the death-haunted, lifeless November nature overwhelmed me as I stood shivering in the cold and humid night. And once again I wondered what strange story Shiva might be able to tell about the mysterious destiny which exiled him to a city of cool bankers, provided his divine Highness would ever condescend speaking to an ordinary mortal like me.

Decades later I discovered in a most unexpected way that the mysterious Hindu god – whose bloodthirsty alter ego relished human sacrifices – had indeed a dark secret to reveal about the way he and his demonic following of exotic idols had found a haven in Zurich's Rietberg Museum. The discovery shattered at the same time my childhood's dream of an innocent and sheltered all-Swiss paradise protected by benevolent fairies and elves.

So far, I had known the Baron von der Heydt – the original owner of Shiva Nataraja, the Lord of the Dance – as a benevolent seeker after the esoteric wisdom of Asia. However, when I was reading a book about Swiss banking, Shiva's tortuous path leading to his Swiss exile became suddenly illuminated as if history's murky dark had been lit up by the dazzling light of a signal flare – and the path so shown was bordered by sinister swastika flags.

Being a rich German citizen, Baron von der Heydt had acted as financial adviser to the German Kaiser, Wilhelm II. In 1926 he acquired the fabled Monte Verità estate as a haven of spiritual enlightenment. But in 1933 he acquired something far less noble: membership in Germany's Nazi party. To be on the safe side, he prudently became a Swiss citizen in 1937, without severing his German ties. During World War II, while I was living in my seemingly innocent Appenzell paradise, Switzerland actually teemed with secret agents of all sorts. Von der Heydt's Locarno bank reportedly was used to funnel funds to a worldwide Nazi spy network. Accused of involvement in foreign intelligence work, the Baron was stripped of his Swiss citizenship immediately after the war.

Things looked even bleaker for the famous art collector when imprisoned German agents admitted to the Americans that they had received money through his Locarno bank, whose owner now also faced a U.S. trial as an enemy agent. Precisely at that time, von der Heydt had lent his famous collection of Oriental treasures to the Buffalo Art Museum. This was the only instance in the war-torn forties when immortal gods and idols were taken hostage instead of ordinary mortals such as French maquisards or Yugoslavian partisans. The Americans, without further ado, sequestered the priceless art collection. Incongruously, this proved to be von der Heydt's salvation.

In a clever move, he transferred the ownership of his collection to Zurich's city fathers, who shrewdly recognized its immense value and were thus eager to grant asylum to lofty foreign gods, in contrast to many Jewish fugitives who had been turned back at the border by Swiss authorities during the war years. Foreign gods apparently had more luck with the Swiss immigration authorities than lowly human beings, even a criminal god like Shiva who unscrupulously had accepted countless human sacrifices during many centuries. In order to defend his position, the Baron also stressed his connection to a mysterious Gestapo official residing in Switzerland, Hans Gisevius, who was alleged to belong to the anti-Hitler resistance movement.

Anyhow, this mysterious affair came to the proverbial happy end. The horde of foreign gods escaped American seizure and took up permanent residence in the stately Wesendonck mansion, providing at the same time the unique ransom which granted again Swiss citizenship to their former owner. And this is why, since 1952, dispassionately meditating Buddhas, serene Chinese sages, grotesque African fetishes, nightmarish South-Sea idols and blood-thirsty Aztec deities permanently hold their silent congregation in the solemnly beautiful Reitberg park, supremely presided by India's Lord of the Dance, Shiva Nataraja, the only four-armed citizen Zurich can boast of.

These foreign gods, brought here by a Nazi-connected financier, have in a sense become more real to me than the elfish deities who vanished together with the enchanted all-Swiss world of my childhood.

Dining Out in Switzerland

by Harold Mac Farland

Looking out through the floor to ceiling window of my hospital room over the smoke-gray Rhine at the smokestacks of the chemical factories to the left and the low brick buildings wrapped in a comfortable blue smoke across the river, I realize I knew the evening was going to go wrong. My Swiss doctors tell me in American English broader than my own that my collapse was precipitated by what I experienced while dining at the Hotel Aeschenkrug.

I was drained and exhausted by the work – and the fun – of the past few months. On the other hand, if it hadn't been for the very unusual atmospheric conditions at the restaurant, I am convinced that I could have scraped through till my vacation next week. As it is, Professor Dr. Rauch believes I'll need at least ten days of rest and special respiratory therapy.

The work: I am a marketing man for Cinder Islands Chemicals here in Switzerland. We specialize in consumer products and medical supplies. I am good at my job, meaning I also have a good team of 15 internationals which I manage pretty well. But for reasons of health, two of the secretaries in our team are incapacitated and the campaign for our new condoms has been murderous the past several weeks. Trips to headquarters, Lyons and New York, of course, have been keeping me busy. The day before yesterday I had to present the five-year budget for my department. I pride myself on doing this very well. In fact, I got the money with no problems – which is why I decided to celebrate with Gaby.

The fun: Gaby is not, as you might have supposed, my wife. My wife's name is Barbara. Gaby is actually my mistress, my second serious girl-friend since I've separated from my wife. If you are interested in beautiful women, and I suppose most are, then I will tell you that Gaby is really all that a man of 40 could desire in a woman:

28, slender legs, chiseled hips, flawless bottom, a beautiful unlined and undefined face – perfect for day and nightdreams; for sweeteners, her bosom is large, firm and convincing. Her nipples are smart; whenever I greet them, they gather themselves up and return the favor as if I were their master, as if they really did recognize me as such. Maybe my girl-friend contributed something to drain on my bio-energy – all too willingly, really – though, of course, she would never have wanted to bring about my collapse last night.

The restaurant: Just off the market-place, a hundred paces from the gilded, rose sandstone Rathaus. The hotel is modern, architected to fit in with its ancient two-story neighbors which are crowned with points and encrusted with shutters. But the cellar is original: a voluminous vaulted room of stone and brick, ribbed with wooden beams beautifully aged by centuries of smoke from the cooking and from the smoking diners.

The menu: A new sensation in town called the "Three worlds"; a 30-course menu – big enough to beat the Chinese at their own game, expensive enough for the richest Japanese to be proud of, novel enough to entice the reticent prides of Swiss gourmets and eager American gourmands, too. I hate people who talk about food rather than eat it. But here, I am making an exception about this, after eating the milk-rice, veal stew and canned California peaches, which the nurse served me in bed.

The hotel meal last night was divided into five groups of five dishes each terminated by an ice, from sherbet to *Glacé Double*. Each group was devoted to specialty cuisines, starting out with a pizza the size and color of a typing teacher's thumbnail (eaten with a specially designed knife and fork on a plate of its own, of course) and concluded by a generous tablespoon of Swiss fries, three postage-stamp-sized pieces of calves' liver moistened by an eye dropper of dark Madeira sauce.

The diners: Well-off professionals like myself with clients and/or beautiful women dressed to the teeth, or rather undressed to wrist-thick waists. Many of their faces I knew, of course, and there were even a few old acquaintances of mine there too. The new waitress, Claudette, slender, a tone awkward, spoke better French than Swiss German, giving me a chance to practice my French, that is, when I wasn't devoting myself to Gaby. The owner told me that since they introduced their superlative menu they had to replace their team three times: the experienced girls had all felt poorly.

The problem: The atmospheric conditions in the restaurant. Just before I collapsed, I learned from the owner/manager that a superefficient ventilation system had been installed when they had introduced their "Three Worlds" menu. I had been feeling funny all day. The two women in my team who were absent are very heavy smokers. (I stopped twelve years ago.) And the other two people in the office were competing with each other – for the dozenth time – to stop smoking; the air in the office had a clear dead saccharine quality to it, and I noticed that Philippe looked extremely peaked and white about the mouth most of the morning. About 11 he fished a paper bag out of his desk drawer and hastened out to the restroom. I felt like Philippe looked, but I put it down to staleness (how ironic!) and forced myself through the rest of the day. After all, I had experienced such discomfort after periods of intense stress but had always been revived by dining out Swiss style.

I work in a suburb of Basle with little industry, crawling with trees and bushes and air which has an ominous sweetish characteristic since the wind prevails from the Black Forest. After talking with the doctors here, I now realize that this too contributed to my "suddenly" talking ill as I did.

At my bachelor-flat:

"Hi, honey. Give me a kiss...mmm...Uh, Gaby. Your kiss tastes different – sort of well, sweetish, different."

"Congratulate me, Thomas. I have stopped smoking! Since this morning!"

"And the apartment smells different too." My stomach was protesting.

"Yes! Isn't it great! I've been airing this whole beautiful day! In no time at all the smoke odor will be completely gone!"

"Well. I suppose..." My vision was cuttingly sharp.

"Let's eat!"

"Yes, darling! I'm dying to get a little of the atmosphere of a good Swiss restaurant. I need it."

"Are you all right, my Mousie?"

"The air at the office was bad...well, different. Maybe too much ozone or something. But once we get to the restaurant I'll revive – I always do."

But once then, I vaguely noticed the altered atmosphere; its unnatural clarity had a penetrating delicacy which affected my nerves without my being able to say just what was bothering me. I thought

the 30-course meal would revive me. But drinking the dry Pfeffinger
white wine, I noticed it tasted particularly pronounced – fruity, fine,
and I could almost taste the grapes, feel the vineyard damp on their
rough skins, smell the oak cask and the earthen floor of the storage
cellar. For a moment I even thought I saw a farm girl I used to know
in its light.

"The wine's bad." I muttered.

"Bad? I think it tastes great!"

"Too pronounced! I can almost picture the hills where it was
planted, and smell the thin vacant air it soaked in."

"Well, it tastes much better to me – but not that good!"

"Good?"

"Well isn't it an almost transcendental experience you're
describing, Mousie?"

"I suppose so...but you know how I dislike the countryside."

"Silly."

Then I noticed a confusion of smells drifting towards our table:
cooked tomato – so sharp and pungent I felt I was bending over the
sauce pot. It reminded me of glorious meals in smoke-filled
restaurants in Italy. But some ingredient was missing and the strength
of the smell made me think of adolescence, sports and underarms –
another area my company is looking into.

An ominous observation: It was at this point I half perceived
something was different about the people at the other tables. But it
wasn't until I had recovered here at the hospital that I began to
assemble a very atypical picture of a Swiss restaurant. I noticed that
most of the couples seemed to be hunched over their tables (not their
plates!) while waiting for the subsequent courses. After we had
munchingly laboured our way through the Indonesian and New
Guinean food groups, I suddenly realized that many of the couples
were holding hands! Very *non comme il faut,* at least among that
clientele.

"Hold my hands, dear!" I entreated Gaby.

"Whatever for? You know I'm not a toucher!"

"Well, sometimes you are."

"But not here! You know how I hate public displays of
emotions."

"Well, you stopped smoking and wouldn't you like to occupy
your hands too?"

"No."

"Gaby, I don't know if I approve of your stopping."

"But YOU stopped!"

"To save money at that time. I just never got back into the habit."

"Just never got back into the habit! If you hadn't started putting all the money you saved into one of your two dozen Swiss bank accounts..."

"All with their own numbers!"

"...you wouldn't be so stingy about it now."

Gaby! Twelve times 365 equals...4380 times let's say 2 francs 50 is...10,950 Swiss francs darling!"

"But you're bulging with money. What are you going to do with it?"

"It's a surprize."

I had planned on surprizing Gaby with an Atmospheric Cities Tour this summer on a sort of pseudo honeymoon instead of the extremely dull, nerve wracking and lung-straining stay under 10,000 umbrellas on the Cote d'Azur or even worse in the garish chlorophylled nature of the Swiss-Italian alps. Now, I'll be using the money for special hospital treatment, including a daily regimen of at least 10 cigarettes a day and more if the same calamitous circumstances should occur again. But more of that later.

"I don't feel too well. The flavor of the food is so salient that it is upsetting me. Is there such a thing as olfactory hallucination?"

"I'm sure I wouldn't know. But you sure don't look too well."

"Everything looks so clear and sharp here tonight, and everybody's holding hands...so unnatural. Even the somber Swiss mutts between the tables aren't their usual perky selves."

"You didn't see the program on TV against smoking last night. You were in Lyons."

"Is that why you stopped again? You know, you smell...well, not bad, but different. I need (how true I was soon to learn!) the smokey smell of your hair, Gaby, and your clothes. Your skin smells like, like, well, people, or woman, no...I know now, like milk...Gaby...like mother's milk." Gaby looked shocked. I realize now that it was here I began to disintegrate. I think I even had the rare experience of seeing my mother's breasts (her "muscles"), smelling the sweetish milk mixed with tomatoey smell of her underarms.

"Mousie..."

I saw spots before my eyes for a moment.

The manager was telling me "...the new ventilation system removes pollution from the air of the restaurant..."

"...pollution?"

"Well, smoke. And adds the amount of oxygen normally to be found, say, in the woods."

"...the woods...?"

"But as you see, after that TV program last night, it's almost superfluous. For the first time in my thirty years of running a restaurant in Switzerland NOT ONE CUSTOMER IS SMOKING – thanks to TV!"

Yes, that was it! Instead of leaning back and enjoying their cigarettes and Cuban cigars, discoursing on auto and god (virtually the same thing to the countrymen of my chosen country), they were entering into uncharacteristic skin-contact with one another!

The climax: I collapsed. Later Gaby told me that my face landed with great force in the gazpacho and covered a lot of the new converts to non-smoking with tomato soup – serves them right! At least the dogs were happy: one man's poison is another dog's treat.

First aid: Would have been, according to Dr. Rauch, puffing strong Swiss cigar smoke into the victim's face and not loosening the collar. But of course the disease is a new one to be added to the list of illness produced by our civilization and I had to be taken to the hospital.

The diagnosis: an insufficient supply of at least one of the 3000 substances contained in cigarette smoke.

The cure: I have to spend ten minutes of every hour in the doctors' lounge (where there is a generous natural supply of tobacco smoke) and will have to gradually start smoking again – this as an emergency measure. The doctors have determined that I am one of a growing number of passive smokers who benefits from cigarette smoke first having passed through others' lungs. I'll have to avoid New York's rabid anti-smoking environs. They have told me that I will have to change my job. For a person with my infirmity, being a waiter in a restaurant with plenty of smoke is about the only profession that'll ensure keeping my present health level.

I accept this, though it'll mean a steep reduction in income. Again for health reasons, I'll probably have to return to my wife! All the younger women are militant non-smokers. Thank god she began smoking heavily when we separated. I'll go back to our modest apartment near one of the smoke emitting chemical factories here, where I always felt better anyway.

I can learn to be a waiter if it means staying alive, but it can't be at the Hotel Aeschenkrug. You'll never find me in that clean air again. It'd be the death of me. And from now on, when we dine out, it will have to be at one of the many old-fashioned, blue-atmosphered restaurants still adorning this smoke-wreathed minster-towered town.

* * * *

For Peter Bosshard, the only restaurant-going Swiss I know
who has given up smoking, and for all non-smokers
who'd like to dine out in Switzerland.

Harold Mac Farland

Belonging

by Kathy Tschurtschenthaler

It started with an announcement in one of our local newspapers over four years ago about a church service on a Friday morning in a home for the elderly nearby. The public was 'welcome'. Having lived in Switzerland's somewhat closed society for almost twenty years, I wondered whether it really meant that just anyone could attend. Since I have a friend whose aunt was in this particular home, I asked if she would join me. After some hesitation, she agreed.

I had recently returned from the States after having to put my own mother in a nursing home there. She was so pleased to have visits from her family. But I also realized that many of her lonely hours were enlightened by the visits of 'volunteers' and I was relieved to know that there would be someone who would visit her from time to time. I could manage to see her only a few weeks a year as could most of my sisters and brothers who also lived long distances from California. Could it be that there were elderly here in Switzerland in the same predicament as my mother? Could I help relieve someone else's loneliness when I couldn't help my own mother?

When we started off that Friday morning, we were not completely sure we were doing the right thing. As we entered the home we felt we were being observed quite closely but we continued to the room where the church service would be held. We were met at the door by the head of the home who was most friendly. We soon realized we were the only non-residents of the home attending the service even though it had been announced every other week in the paper with a note that the public was invited. My friend and I were the only 'public'.

After the service I suddenly felt a hand on my arm and then slowly another arm hooked into mine. I no longer felt like a stranger. We continued to attend the church service every other week as the only 'public' and soon I started stopping in to say hello to my new friend there. Slowly many of the other residents started to greet me as my presence became more familiar to them. I began to enjoy going there whenever I could to say hello or take someone for a walk. I felt very fortunate to be able to spend many of my new friend's last hours holding her hand and letting her know she was not alone.

Photo SNTO.

That was how it started. I am still attending the church services and visit whenever I can. Many of the original faces are gone now but there are others whose families are scattered or have no family. Recently I was asked to help with the home's activation therapy program. Though I have always felt very much at home in Switzerland, I now feel I am an accepted member of the community. Many others are needed to become small links in a long chain which could reach around the world and help relieve the loneliness of the aged and infirmed.

Kathy Tschurtschenthaler

Some Unforgettable Experiences

by Dianne Dicks

One of my most embarrassing experiences in Switzerland occured only a few days after my arrival. That was over twenty-five years ago but I recall the scene vividly as if it were yesterday and the recollection still makes me squirm uncomfortably.

It was my very first venture out alone in Basle. On an exchange program, I had travelled to Switzerland with a group of Americans. The Swiss family I was to spend the summer with had met me at the train station upon my arrival just a few days before. They had been extremely hospitable and had taken great care to show me around Basle by car and by tram. That particular day I decided I could not expect them to 'entertain' me with a program every day and that I could easily go into Basle by tram for some sight-seeing on my own.

Most of the trams then did not have automatic doors. During rush hours they burst with people. I thought I was lucky when the most modern tram model rolled up to my tram stop. It not only had automatic doors, but the man taking tickets was seated at the back behind a counter. I was glad about that as I had been afraid that the friendly ticket takers would want to chatter with me as they did on the older model trams while making their way through the tram to collect fares from the passengers. I was relieved to see the new shiny tram and a ticket taker seated behind a counter from which I could quickly escape after showing my ticket without having to say a word.

I didn't mind the crowd, in fact, somehow I felt so conspicuous as if my appearance alone made it evident to the world that I did not speak a word of German, let alone the unusual dialect spoken in Basle. I glanced around the tram and when my eyes met the gaze of the Helvetia-like woman sitting across from me, I smiled a nervous but meaningless smile in greeting as I might have done on a bus back home in Indianapolis. I learned that one obviously doesn't smile at strangers on trams. She looked away quickly, pretending not to see me – I must have embarrassed her terribly as she rigidly stared out of the window, never daring to glance my way again.

Travelling by tram was simple enough even in those days but to me, all alone in my first strange country, it was the wildest adventure I had ever had. I had intended to count the stops so that I would know where to get off. It should have been 9 stops. Suddenly I realized that I had not been counting properly since the tram also stopped at a few red lights. Instantly, in panic that I was already lost, I jumped up to get closer to the door so that I could get off the tram more quickly once I recognized my destination. The tram was terribly crowded and it was difficult to make my way to the door. I didn't know what to say to get people to step aside a bit so that I could pass by and I was afraid to utter anything at all for fear of being spotted as a foreigner and a complete fool for not knowing any German.

Once I finally reached the doorway, I thought I recognized a few buildings of the fair grounds and I was relieved that I still had a few stops to go. With each stop the tram grew more crowded until we were all packed like sardines. I clutched my handbag. It was impossible to avoid touching the other passengers as the tram rolled along the tracks, swaying its way around curves and jolting every so slightly with every start and stop. In spite of my nervous state, I remembered to avoid eye contract and restrain my nervous Indiana smile.

Then it happened. He was behind me. I couldn't see his face. He had been talking in my ear. I could just sense that he was addressing me – to me his voice left no doubt about his intentions. I looked quickly at the other passengers, hoping someone would notice the danger I was in of being molested. Surely someone would, and come to my rescue and tell the nerd off. To my surprise no one seemed to care. Nobody paid any attention.

He whispered "Squeeze me." I probably turned blue from embarrassment and fright. I had become so nervous that on top of everything else, I didn't realize how many stops the tram had made.

"Squeeze me, Fräulein." This time he addressed me quite openly and I became even more embarrassed and unable to turn around and give him the dirty look I knew he deserved.

"Squeeze ME!" He had the nerve to even get angry. I looked around at the other passengers and to my horror they were all staring at me! What strange people! I had heard of the decadence of morals in Europe, but I had never expected to be molested in broad daylight in Switzerland. The moment the tram's automatic doors opened at the next stop, I flew out. To my horror, he got out too. No one else had got out of the tram! It's door closed automatically and it rolled off leaving me stranded with a monster.

Clutching my bag, I flashed around to give him a look that would kill. To my surprise, he was walking away from me, shaking his head. He never looked back.

I walked in the direction the tram had disappeared, just a stop or two and found myself at the Marktplatz in the center of Basle from where my shopping excursion was to begin. I was shaken from the experience but determined to make the best of a lovely sunny afternoon in this quaint town. Occasionally I shuddered, recalling his first crude whispers in my ear, "Squeeze me." I knew I had been lucky and since there was no reason to cause a scandal, I decided to say nothing about it to my host family.

A few days later while I was washing dishes in the kitchen of my Swiss family with my Swiss 'mother', the Swiss 'father' came into the kitchen with his arms full of papers to be thrown away.

He stood at the sink beside me and said, "Squeeze me!"

I flashed a look of surprise at him.

He repeated without the slightest hesitation, "Squeeze me!"

I looked at his wife. She explained, "The garbage can is under the sink. He just wants you to step aside."

I not only stepped aside, I sat down and thought through the whole affair. "Why did you say 'squeeze me', Arnold?"

"I didn't say 'squeeze me', I said 'èxgyysi', that's Basle dialect for 'excuse me'. Why? Is something wrong?"

* * * *

Over the years I've invested quite a lot of time and money in learning German. My version of it is now quite fluent, at least it seems that way to me. I haven't the slightest problem expressing myself and I'm rarely misunderstood by the natives even though my Hoosier twang mingled into it might leave a few aghast. When I'm in Germany I hear, "Oh, what a funny Swiss accent you have!" Here in Basle, "Where did you learn to speak German like that?"

The last time I was in the States the cab driver taking us into Manhattan from Kennedy airport was fascinated how I was translating all his comments into my version of German for my children in the back seat. New York cabbies are notorious and hearing him speak was like music to my ears after having been abroad so many years.

After a while he asked "Where do you folks come from?"

"Well, they're from Switzerland, but actually I'm an American."

"Ah, lady, come on, don't give me that stuff. With an accent like that! You're pulling my leg!" I felt like telling him to take me back to Kennedy.

One of the first things my family always says to me when I get back to the States is how I sound like a foreigner.

Frankly, I'm sick of the topic. Not too long ago I went into a supermarket in Basle just to get a liter of milk and while I was paying for it, the cashier latched on to me at my mere mumble of the customary *'merci viel mal'* (thanks). Hearing my accent made her very curious and extremely friendly. She didn't stop asking questions

Foreigners are easily detected in Switzerland by their accents when pronouncing tongue-tangling places. Photo SNTO.

and I had to tell her the story of my life. I love talking to people but I'm so tired of those same old questions that invariably come up after I've said just a few words.

The answer to the problem would obviously be to weed out the most striking reverberations in my various languages. Speech training would do the trick. I've wanted to do it for years. The problem is first deciding upon what version of German I want to speak. Nobody would want to speak to me anymore in Basle if I spoke perfect German. Nobody speaks perfect German anyway.

Every time I'm determined to learn proper Basle dialect, I'm told conflicting things about its grammar and pronunciation. If these people can't agree how it is to be spoken properly, why should it make such a difference if I plop in a High German word here and pepper it with English there?

Since I have obviously developed an aversion to some of the nit-picking of linguists, it is a surprize to many people that I can actually enjoy teaching English. My students know I respect them, however their words come out. I do feel sorry for anyone having to learn another language. There are some rules in English books that no self-respecting English-speaking native would ever use. Can you imagine asking "Usen't there to be trees here?" That question was part of an exercise to practice 'used to'. I still haven't found anyone who can confidently tell me how to answer it – "No, there usen't" or "Yes, there usen't" both sound pretty terrible to me. Why do students have to practice such nonsense? Teaching them to talk with their hands and feet would be much less embarrassing for everybody and do more to promote good communication.

As far as proper English goes, I received a few lessons from my English au-pairs. Sharing a common language often stood in the way of our understanding each other. The misunderstandings were always delightful and we had a lot of fun trying to translate our Englishes to each other. Jackie would say "Wot toime d'ya moik it?" when she wanted to ask about the time and I always thought she wanted me to guess the time. I'd look up in the air and say, "Oh, I'd say about 3." She'd get upset and say, "Well, loik at yr wotch!" I tried to teach her to say "What time is it?" but to no avail. We had the same problem again during our farewells at the airport after her year was over. My 5-year-old daughter told her with tears in her eyes. "I hope you noiver choinge." So do I.

The worst thing about speaking your own version of a language is that you can never win an argument. People just don't take you seriously if you have any kind of accent – they'll be consoling, supporting, understanding and tolerant but you can tell by the twinkle in their eye that you're just a joke to them.

* * * *

I worked a number of years in a Swiss insurance company. Among other things I also taught English. Our classes always started at 8 o'clock and I made a point of never being late. One such morning, on the way to work, I got tied up in a real sticky traffic jam and arrived at the office only at 9:15. My students had been concerned and had called my boss to inquire about me. My office mates had received innumerable calls from people wanting to reach me. With these three men in the office I explained, still out of breath from dashing from the garage, that there had been a lot of traffic – in German 'Verkehr' – and that the whole town was one big traffic jam.

Just then, the sex bomb of the office waddled in, high heels and all. She was also out of breath and I turned to her innocently and asked in German, "Miss Muller, did you also have a lot of traffic this morning?" In German 'Verkehr' also means sexual intercourse and my *"Haben Sie auch viel Verkehr heute morgen gehabt?"* was misunderstood and she was quite stunned at my openness. While the three men were laughing themselves into hysterics, I tried to straighten it out with her by explaining what I had meant to say.

It certainly shook my confidence in my German but the episode must have cheered up a lot of offices for awhile. The story got around. A few hours later someone working in a pharmaceutical firm in Basle called to tell me that 'Verkehr' story, with a few small details added here and there of course. I still don't know how I could have said it differently without being misunderstood. Probably if a German-speaking person had said the same thing, it would not have been misconstrued. But then, we wouldn't have had such a good laugh.

From Rags to Linguistics

by Lilliam Hurst-Garbutt

I was born in Central America, Costa Rica to be precise, because my parents, who were poor, indigenous missionaries in a small Protestant Denomination, had been transferred there three months before my birth. When I use the word 'poor', I use it very advisedly indeed, for they were both of modest stock – fisherfolk on my father's side of the family in British Honduras, and simple peasants scrabbling for a living in Managua, where they should never have ended up in the first place. Of course, the very idea of America, or Europe were like foreign notions to us, and we never expected any of us would actually ever end up there! My cousins were all doing exciting things like sewing hems on dishrags, or working as civil servants in Belize City.

We moved from five houses in four cities before I was 6. My family was transferred to Panama, Barbados, and Trinidad before my father retired early in order to take my three brothers, my sister and me to California "for the children's education," as he said. He had only 'retired', however, to take on two jobs so that he could pay for our schooling.

Then, while I was attending a small denominational College in Riverside, California, I was given the opportunity of going away for a year abroad. My dad calculated the cost of this very carefully, then gave me his go-ahead. The school was just outside Geneva, on the low mountain called "The Salève". I spent two years there, with ups and downs, but improving my command of French daily.

After the two years were up, I regretfully returned to California to obtain my B.A. During my senior year I attended a conference on linguistics upon the recommendation of my French professor. I had always been fascinated by language – we spoke Spanish and English at home and I had picked up French along the way too so I guess I was fertile ground for that lecture. During the evening, the lecturer spoke about Ferdinand de Saussure, the Father of Modern Linguistics who I learned had lived and worked in Geneva.

The college encouraged me to get some useful experience 'elsewhere' and then return to the college as a teaching assistant. I decided to go back to Geneva for graduate work in linguistics. I was able to meet their grade requirements but I was left with the problem of financing. I called on Dad. He had been unable to complete a formal education, and had taught himself most of what he knew, but for him nothing was as important as an advanced education. He hadn't the foggiest notion of what linguistics was about. I knew only what our lecturer had said in that one evening session, but I decided to give it a try. It was decided that I would work during the summer, as I always had, and that he would then send me, royally $50.00 a month and I would just have to make do with that! Famous last words...

I kept my side of the bargain and worked like mad during the summer. When I arrived in Geneva, I at once started to read everything I could lay my hands on, but haphazardly – reading a chapter from Leonard Bloomfield, followed by another by Edward Sapir, and a little Noam Chomsky to finish me off. Things were getting more and more confused. I wondered how I would ever manage. I did notice a blond young man looking over the top of his book with some insistence, but I wasn't in Geneva for any hanky-panky, I was here for linguistics, so I carried on plowing through the Bloomfield, Sapir et al.

When the semester started, I set off for my first linguistics class. It was to be given by the spiritual grandson, so to speak, of the great Ferdinand de Saussure himself: Henri Frei. I walked in to the first session and saw the most wrinkled old wizard I had ever laid eyes on. He looked about a hundred years old to my twenty-year-old eyes (he was in fact 67), and he had this tiny, frail voice that you simply couldn't hear if you weren't actually sitting right at the front of the class like I did. We had a two-hour lesson each time, and during the second hour his voice got weaker and weaker. His hair, dyed to a Venetian-blond tint, had snow-white roots which were touched up periodically by his wife, but never soon enough to avoid our eagle eyes. In his quavering voice he commenced to explain the arcane mysteries of linguistics, and we soon forgot he was old, we stopped looking at his roots, and all scribbled furiously, trying to understand as we wrote. We were to discover that we were in the presence of a great man.

Professor Frei became more and more tired as the end of the two-hour sessions of his 'ex cathedra' course approached. We could hardly hear what he was saying, to say nothing of understanding. Another classmate and I took turns rushing down to the cafeteria, buying a double-strength coffee, rushing back up and offering it to him. Then we could all sit back and wait for a new Henri Frei to appear. He was always wide awake during the second hour after that, with a much stronger voice.

In the meantime, the young man in the library had introduced himself. When the time came at the end of the year for me to return to my job in California, I discovered that what I wanted, after all, was to stay in Geneva, continue my degree here, and especially, fit in wherever André was.

In order to better 'fit in', I spoke to André mainly in French, and this was also because, at the time, he was not comfortable speaking English. I was to half-regret this later. I suspect that the slight embarrassment that André appeared to feel whenever I spoke English in public (as if my French weren't good enough, even though it was) may have played a part in the relative lack of use of my mother-tongue during that brief period of my life.

André is a classical philologist and he introduced me to Robert Godel who was a Latinist and specialist of Armenian Linguistics and author of various books on grammar. Godel undertook to guide my reading in linguistics much more systematically so that my understanding of the course began to be better. My gratitude to him is enormous. To many people, Robert Godel appeared as a misanthropic don, but with me he was endlessly patient, a kindly father-figure with clear explanations, a vast store of books to lend, and most important, in Geneva, where people are said to be cold and distant, he had an open-door policy.

Geneva is not very big as cities go, but the presence of all the international organizations makes it appear more cosmopolitan and more of a metropolis than it really is. As in all old cities, there is a well-established aristocracy and a relatively self- protective gentry. The fact that there are so many foreigners has exacerbated this need for self-protection. It seemed necessary either to have such a background of your own in your own country in order to impress the 'natives' into submission (as the many Russian princes-in-exile had done), or to arrive with a portfolio full of financial clout to dazzle the secret banker lurking in the heart of so many Genevese. I had neither, and had André not been my passport into his circle of friends, I would most certainly not have been able to build up one of my own as widely or as quickly as I did. The Genevese, I was to discover, deserved the reputation of being close and difficult to get to know, particularly if they felt that you might not be appreciating their city as much as they thought you should be. As André's companion, I was not being subjected to the same initiation rites as some of my foreign classmates who were promised invitations which then never took place.

The problem of language was becoming tricky. I had done all my previous schooling in English, and all of a sudden, I was trying to discuss arcane points about French with people of French mother-tongue, in French, and in the presence of luminaries such as Robert Godel and Henri Frei. It was enough to give anyone's self-confidence a jolt, particularly mine. As I was doing my degree in French literature, with Jean Rousset and Jean Starobinski (Geneva was full of luminaries!), I was assumed to be perfectly assimilated and capable in French. I wasn't helped by the fact that when I went in to the 'practical phonetics' courses, it took a kymograph (a complex apparatus with all manner of ways of measuring speech production, such as an 'olive' up a nostril, one airstream-sensitive microphone suspended before one's lips, a melody graph and another vibration-sensitive microphone attached over the larynx) to detect the slightest trace of a 'foreign' accent in my French.

I felt I was becoming somewhat disjointed language-wise, because it was considered as 'natural' by all those around me that I should henceforth renounce the claim of English on my thought-processes. I found that hard to accept.

My thoughts were not only on linguistics but turned to romance. André and I got married. I found myself with a Swiss passport, a Swiss husband and a home for the future. I had never thought that would happen to me! The idea of having one country to live in for the foreseeable future was what brought about the greatest change in my way of thinking. Before that, I had always known that I would be leaving in two or three years, so I had never tried to establish roots.

After a number of years, our first daughter arrived. We named her Samia, for linguistic reasons – my maternal grandmother, still alive at the time, spoke only Spanish, my father's family only English, André's extended family only Swiss-German, and our friends in Geneva spoke mainly French. We needed a name that would not be irreparably altered every time our little girl was called in to supper. I, of course, spoke to her in English, because the words came more easily in my own language, and because I wanted her to be able to speak with her grandparents on my side. For the first year and a half of her life it was a cinch – I spoke to her in English all the time, and in French to everyone else.

I had very few friends of English mother-tongue because, in trying to fit in, I had also tried to fit in linguistically. I had not sought out the expatriate English-speaking community in Geneva which would have provided a vast pool of allies. So I was always shifting from English to French, every time I had to speak to the butcher, the baker, or anyone else, and back again when when I spoke to Samia. After her first words in English, then her first phrases, she began to answer me in French. She didn't see why only she was addressed in English. Of course, the presence of her French-speaking Daddy, Grandmaman, and so on didn't help my cause any. After a while, I became convinced that I might do her 'linguistic' harm if I continued to insist that she stand out so singularly from the crowd. I began to give in, using English words once in a while to say things I couldn't say in French easily – family words from my own childhood, words I found funny in English but not in French, and so on. For example, because of her plump cheeks, we always called her 'cheeky', long before she was able to try her hand at being cheeky! This doesn't work in French. These words became the sum of Samia's English vocabulary, not much to build on, but better than nothing. After our second daughter, Vanessa, arrived, I continued to speak French because it was expected of me. But inwardly, I began to resent more and more that I was being torn from a whole aspect of my past experiences.

In 1981, when Samia was about ten, André was due a Sabbatical and, after some hesitation, decided to spend his six months' leave at St. John's College, Oxford. The girls would attend school there and I would remain in Oxford alone with them when André had to return to Geneva at the end of his sabbatical. There are no special courses for non-English speakers in state schools in Britain, but our girls did just beautifully even though their English was virtually non-existent. For what earthly use could the baby words they knew be to them on the playgrounds of St. Nicholas' First School and Harlow Middle School? Once they had the rudiments, however, they progressed by leaps and bounds – it was as if their ears, having been accustomed to the sounds of English, even if only episodically, had taught their minds and tongues to use English once they were given the opportunity.

After our return to Geneva, we established a rule that they speak to me exclusively in English, even if they continued to use French with their father. It was useful for them to have an adult French-speaking model to counter the influence of the increasingly slangy French being spoken in school. After that, they were sent off to England every summer to stay with friends or families recommended to us by those friends, or even to 'Activity Camps'. Each time I accompanied them to drop them off, I rediscovered the joy of knowing that all day I would be speaking English, only English, with all the zest of one deprived of this possibility for so long.

Samia's acceptance into the anglophone section of her English classes at school, her subsequent marks in English, the compositions she can now write, have made me mouth the Anglican prayer for the ends of meals: "For what we have just received, may the Lord make us truly thankful." Vanessa's growing up with some of the same possibilities, my being able to share jokes in English with both of them and their being able to understand my family when we go for a visit are all sources of profound satisfaction to me as a mother. I feel that, aside from having passed on the genes that have made them what they are, I have also been able to pass on a small portion of cultural heritage, fragmentary though it may be.

Had I not followed the route that I did, I might be sewing zig-zag seams around the edges of dishrags today. I do not have the impression that I intentionally tried to leave that part of my life behind. Every decision I made from the age of nine when I decided to learn French seems to have led me along the road to Switzerland.

No-bang Fawkes

by Tony Obrist

It you want to let off fireworks in Switzerland on any occasion other than the Swiss national holiday, August 1, you need a permit from the police. The landlady of my first digs in Basle told me this when I recounted my plan for a small display to celebrate my engagement. November 4 was my intended's birthday, and I had managed to persuade my future in-laws to postpone the celebration by a day.

I had been starved of fireworks in my childhood in Britain during the War, when the only activity of this nature had been provided by courtesy of Herr Hitler – very spectacular at times, to be sure, but where was the fun when you couldn't light the blue touch paper yourself? Later, with the world at peace again, I was one of the postgraduate chemistry students whose research suddenly required supplies of potassium chlorate as October drew to a close. The storekeeper saw through this at once, of course, and made appropriately snide remarks; but the indent had been countersigned by the research supervisor, who was as keen as any of the students, so there was nothing he could do about it. Except for the few we tried out in the yard at the back of the building, the fireworks we made were, however, destined for the students' 'official' celebration, which I wasn't able to stay on for because the last train to my home in the suburbs ran too early.

It has been my lifelong conviction that fireworks are the apotheosis of the chemist's art. Hence my desire to have some on that first, memorable, Fifth of November in Switzerland.

A permit? No problem, said my landlady; she knew somebody at police headquarters who would fix it. But it proved to be something even she couldn't fix. I should have to call at headquarters personally, she was told. No sooner said than done. I was received politely by an elderly official, who listened attentively to my account of the Gunpowder Plot and seemed relieved when I said I did not contemplate more than two rockets, and no bangers. He wanted to know exactly where and at what time I had in mind. That would be all right, he said finally; the permit would arrive by post in a few days.

But no, there was more to come. My polite policeman rang me a little later at the office. He needed some additional facts. He knew (he said) that Fawkes meant fireworks in English, but it was this "Gwee" (as he pronounced it) that he wasn't sure about. So I put him right on Guy Fawkes as gently as I could. Ah yes, he said, he knew all that, of course, but was just checking up. And indeed, the permit arrived a few days later, as you see it here. As my friendly policeman is probably now patrolling the Great Beat in the Sky, I have concealed his name, but otherwise it is just as I received it. I thought it worth preserving. One astonishing feature is that there was no charge for it

Photo SNTO.

— Swiss officials usually have a supply of adhesive stamps of various denominations which they stick on documents and cancel to make them cost something. Perhaps the case was so unusual that there was no appropriate denomination in stock.

Armed with my permit I went along to Franz Carl Weber — at that time, apart from the two joke and conjuring shops, the only shop in Basle that sold fireworks. It was an experience in itself. I was taken up onto the roof, where the remnant stock from August 1 was kept in an iron strongroom. Joyfully I selected my two rockets and was careful to ensure that their non-explosive nature was certified on the sales slip, as you can see. Having made fireworks myself I knew the surprises they can give you, and I didn't want to be accused of violating the terms of my permit.

After all that, I am happy to report that the fireworks (and the engagement) were a great success. At 8.00 p.m. precisely on Friday, November 5, they went off without a hitch. No doubt at 7.58 the sergeant at the Badischer Bahnhof local police station (where a copy of the permit had been sent by headquarters) said to his sidekick, "Time to check the fireworks, Charlie," and, reaching down for his fur cap, binoculars and stopwatch, stomped out with him to scan the winter sky and listen for forbidden detonations. I do hope they enjoyed the show as much as we did.

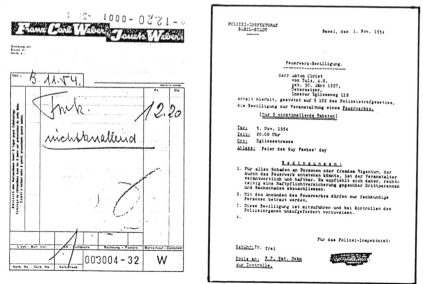

Culture Shock

by Jacob Christ

Culture shock is associated with moving from one country or culture to another. It can occur shortly after arrival in the new country or show up after some time. It has long been known that people experience stress when moving to a new country. When this also involves coping with a different language, the stress experienced rates high on a stress scale devised by social psychiatrists studying the effect of crises in life.

Culture shock is a relatively new term. It was coined by those observing the intricacies of the human mind or emotions in the context of the much-increased mobility of intellectual cadre and middle-management-level workers for the multinational companies, the increased international exchange of scientists, engineers and business people and, of course, the resulting increasing number of trans-cultural marriages.

Being a tourist or travelling on short visits to another country provokes quite a different experience. One may end up in embarrassing situations or annoying circumstances when one does not know the language of the country visited, but an experience of real culture shock is rare under those circumstances. A tourist is out to see the beautiful sights and ordinarily passes his or her time in a state of mild euphoria, living and later re-living the trip with the help of slides or photographs. There was no intention to work in the country visited, nor to stay.

Switzerland has a long tradition of creating enthusiasm among English-speaking tourists, especially the Americans or English, who may happily anticipate a longer stay in such a beautiful place. When being relocated for a longer time in Switzerland, their feeling of disappointment is much greater than expected and the realities of adaptation to Swiss language and culture seem overwhelming.

Culture shock has a lot to do with 'alienation', also a relatively new word which, like *Entfremdung* in German, refers to feeling like a stranger to oneself or to being estranged, not belonging to a group and not having a purpose. This feeling of having no purpose in the new country may also seem quite irrational since it contradicts the solid knowledge that one has come to work for a company, for one's

On the way to the vet in the valley by helicopter. Photo SNTO.

research project or one's own business. Alienation is much more of a feeling – an uneasy one at that – than a concrete idea. It is likely to render the sufferer a downcast, sad and lonely person, in spite of the real circumstances which may not be ideal but often quite tolerable.

Sufferers from culture shock or alienation try to find explanations for their sorry state of mind. They can find them either inside themselves or by complaining about their surroundings. If fault is found in themselves, they will claim some personal psychological conflicts or some mental symptoms like depression and they may even seek out treatment with a psychiatrist or counsellor. If, on the other hand, fault is found with the surroundings, they will criticise the host country severely for its reprehensible customs and its people for being difficult to understand.

I can offer an anecdote here from the time when even I suffered from culture shock without knowing what it was. The setting was then not Switzerland, but New York, where I had moved as a 26-year-old Swiss. I could speak very little English at the time and was feeling utterly lost between the skyscrapers, in a citiscape cast in grey. I had the feeling that all this was not real and that I, myself, and my tasks, were no longer quite real. It seemed as if I were not the same person as before. Since I had already begun work in psychiatry, I was able to diagnose 'derealization' and 'depersonalization' in myself which I knew under certain circumstances could be early signs of insanity. Fortunately it passed and I did not become insane.

Since that time, however, I have seen many people under similar circumstances who describe their culture shock, indicating various symptoms of mental or emotional disease. Most often such a person expresses having depressive feelings – much to his or her own surprise. There may also be feelings of helplessness, inferiority or inadequacy, or other moods never before experienced. Sometimes there is increased sensitivity to criticism or a feeling of being looked at disapprovingly by others.

Such a person may become uncharacteristically critical of everything in the new country, even suffering from decidedly paranoid feelings of being thwarted or persecuted. Everything seems to be wrong with the host country – from the apartment provided by the company, to the local telephone system, shopping opportunities or the general unfriendliness of people. Disappointment about the move to a supposedly beautiful, clean and civilized country is then complete. The sufferer starts pondering over typical culture shock questions: "What am I doing here anyway? Why have I come here? How can I bear to stay any longer?"

All these rather menacing symptoms are not signs of mental illness, nor are they reason to pack one's bags and return home. That all this is an adjustment-reaction syndrome belonging to culture shock is sometimes recognized by physicians or psychiatrists, sometimes not.

The family doctor may prescribe some tranquilizing medication and reassure the sufferer that all this is due to nervousness which will in time take care of itself. A psychiatrist or psychologist may try to find emotional disturbances related to previous situations. Effective help will hardly be obtainable from these doctors since the treatment required is not medical nor even psychiatric. Drugs are of little use and talking about one's childhood difficulties is not as useful as it can be in psychotherapy for a neurosis.

What is useful is to help persons suffering from culture shock to get involved in some part of their own home culture again – especially by keeping in contact in the host country with people from the same country of origin who have, at least, the same mother-tongue.

Let's look, as an example, at the case of a woman who has recently moved from an American middle-class suburb to accompany her professional husband to a city like Basle. Whether she is aware of it or not, she has experienced a great loss – usually a loss of family members, of friends and neighbors with whom she had always had contact and from whom she had received support and companionship in many day-to-day activities. It is also a loss not to be able to visit the familiar stores in town where she knew the people and in turn was known by them and greeted in a friendly way. All this is gone now. Instead, there is loneliness; she knows nobody and nobody knows her. These unexpected emotions may be happening to her for the first time in her life and her reaction may come as an entirely unexpected development since she had been looking forward to the move.

Besides experiencing this loss is the confrontation with a new and seemingly impossible-to-learn language. Compound this with the problem of finding new friends, neighbors and contacts. Whether we realize it or not, our language is very much part of our sense of self, our identity and our self-esteem. We express ourselves through our language. When our own language is useless or invalidated, we may easily invalidate ourselves, particularly when we are dependent on the outside world for help in relocating and readjusting. In this predicament of not understanding and of not being understood, our never-before-experienced feelings of inferiority and helplessness can be quite upsetting.

Employees should of course be well-prepared by their companies for a stay in a foreign country by receiving all necessary information and support. Yet even the best preparation and the best of intentions cannot prepare someone for such an emotional reaction – for the culture shock and resulting disorientation. If until now a person has always felt secure and well-adjusted, he or she will find the occurrence of alienation and culture shock most unfamiliar. Before arriving in Switzerland, most of our culture shock victims were normal and well-adjusted people who had previously never been possible candidates for psychotherapy. Most had been supposedly even well-prepared for the experience of an extended stay away from home and had not the slightest idea that anything of this sort could ever happen to them.

How does a culture shock victim deal with the loss of all supports from home and with the loneliness coming from not feeling understood? I have observed two different reactions. Either the victims put the blame on themselves and experience symptoms of an emotional nature like depression, depersonalization or alienation. They may even reject their former identity and sever all connections with the past. Or the victims blame others for the difficulties, making accusations about the host country, whose culture they cannot accept. In the latter case, the actual way of suffering may have an advantage, at least in the long run, and one's suffering does not remain unheard. The victim may encounter disbelief, denials or arguments from the exponents of the host country providing at least an opportunity to test the reality of perceptions and to gradually come to a more balanced view of things. These victims who gripe and accuse may find a piece of truth on their side and this provokes better argumentation and leads to improved self-esteem. In time, such victims may gradually realize that their exaggerated feelings may have been primarily due to culture shock.

Although they are most friendly to tourists, the Swiss are not known to be particularly hospitable to foreigners living in their country. However, culture shock can occur even under the best of circumstances and in the most hospitable of host countries in any culture. Feeling uprooted from one's own culture, experiencing loss and the feeling of not being understood can occur when one immigrates to any country.

One particular Swiss attitude deserves mention here. Any foreigner who comes to live here for some time must adapt to Swiss ways and life styles. Even though this may seem obvious, it is not necessarily like this in other countries. Americans living in Japan for a year or two are not expected to learn Japanese, nor are they expected to take up Japanese customs and ways of life. The British colonial people in India did not need to learn the Indian languages. Western executives in the Middle East can continue to live in their habitual way, though contained in a kind of ghetto.

Americans coming to live in Switzerland cannot easily continue to live as Americans even though they have immigrated into another, even similar Western culture. At least some elements of the language must be learned and a willingness to abide by Swiss ways must be shown – otherwise the immigrant will remain isolated. Complaints about a host-country's habits and customs are never well received by its citizens. This adaptational pressure is definitely stronger in Switzerland than it is in some other European countries.

Another often unexpected difficulty of new arrivals in Switzerland is that German-speaking Switzerland is a land where so-called 'diglossia' prevails. This means that there are always two separate languages in use. One is for writing, namely the German that is taught in schools, read in books and spoken in Germany and Austria. The other language is for speaking and is called *Schwyzerdütsch*, Swiss-German or according to location, Basle, Berne or Zurich German. The Swiss are unable to agree on how to write their spoken Swiss-German because of the variety of local dialects. Besides this, they are reluctant to speak High German, their written language, which is also the language of Germany. When speaking to an English-speaking person, most Swiss prefer to speak English, if they can, rather than High German. Therefore a limited knowledge of German will not be of much help to a newcomer and the circumstances could be particularly disappointing to someone who has made an effort to learn German before coming to Switzerland. These communication difficulties undermine newcomers' adaptational efforts, put them at a disadvantage and reveal the underlying mixed feelings Swiss have concerning outsiders.

Whatever the elements are that may enhance culture shock, it is a stress reaction of an individual who has been hitherto a normal person. In contrast to acute culture shock, the long-term adaptational difficulty that exists for example with foreign 'guest-workers' is most often manifested by psychosomatic symptoms, that is, bodily complaints for which no bodily cause can be found. These symptoms are due to stress, in their case, chronic stress, of being uprooted from their own culture, the experience of losing their own culturally sanctioned ways of conducting life, the loss of the ways they feel family members should live with each other and, above all, the loss of those left behind who can only rarely be visited on vacation. The victims feel misunderstood, not only in terms of the language but in wider emotional sense. Each has landed in an empty space between two cultures: in the host country a 'guest-worker' and foreigner, eventually, when back in the home country, alienated from the family or previous culture because of having been away for an extended period. These chronically stressed individuals share with the acute culture shock victims a history of normality during childhood and young adult life and the cultural uprooting upon immigrating into a new country. In the long run feelings of depression and low self-esteem complicate the picture.

The adaptation of immigrants into a new country has been extensively studied in the United States and Canada. There is general agreement that the stress of immigration is high. Yet surprisingly, foreign immigrants are seen rarely at mental health facilities or in psychiatric hospitals. They seem to deal with the initial culture shock in a different way. The outstanding sociological feature on the American continent is the existence of the so-called 'ethnic ghetto'. In all the larger cities there are neighborhoods populated by members of one or perhaps two ethnic groups. Best known are the Chinatowns and Little Italys, but there are also German, Polish, Eastern Jewish, Puerto Rican and several other ethnic neighborhoods. The connotation of the 'ghetto' is regarded as negative, yet from a point of view of facilitating the adaptation to a new country, the ghetto may well be very helpful. If one is permitted to live at first among people 'from the old country' who speak a familiar language, one buys time for the process of adaptation. Adjustment to the new home country can proceed much more slowly and, for many immigrants to the United States, it may take one entire generation to make the transition from the European to the American culture. The voluntary ghetto may then shelter the newcomers up to a point from a too brutal kind of culture shock.

The 'guest-worker' in Northern Europe is in a somewhat different situation. For one thing the move from the Mediterranean countries to the North was not usually a deliberate decision to leave home and immigrate into a different or better country as it had been in the great waves of immigration to America in the 19th and early 20th centuries. The contemporary foreign worker merely drifts away, perhaps for a year or two as he sees it at first, in order to make some money and return home afterwards. As the distances are not that large, there is no real decision for emigration necessary. Once he has arrived in the host country, there is also very little desire to adapt to that country, as he plans to depart again within a few years. In this way the foreign workers, particularly if they stay for a longer time, gradually lose touch with their home culture and also do not accept the culture of the host country as their own. In this regard they are different from the Europeans who immigrated to America, eager to embrace American culture and habits, acquiring citizenship within five years and in time proud to be Americans. Such immigrants can expect to be almost free of the symptoms of chronic culture shock.

It is very likely that this difference in cultural commitment accounts for the difference in the frequency of stress disorders between bona fide immigrants who have decided to adapt and guest workers who are in the host country without any real desire to belong to it. Both groups eventually lose touch with their original culture, but the immigrant has something to substitute for it – the new culture – whereas the foreign worker falls, so to speak, between two chairs.

How is this non-disease of acute or long-term culture shock treated? The most important 'therapy' to culture-shocked individuals is a piece of their home culture to relieve their feelings of being isolated and belonging nowhere. By having contact with others in the same predicament, this self-help can also become mutual help. English-speaking persons are under as much pressure to adapt in Switzerland as other foreign workers are, yet there also needs to be some room for continuing some interests from 'back home' too. There should be times when the newcomer can speak English without this fact alone attracting attention. Besides having an opportunity to discuss observations and complaints regarding the host country, there must be an opportunity to receive and feel support from fellow men and women in the same position.

There are many English-speaking organizations in Switzerland where ways of obtaining help can be found in coping with culture shock. These English-speaking groups and activities can save potential culture shock victims from excessive suffering and help them to identify the real issues without extensive psychological treatment ever becoming necessary.

Jacob Christ. Photo C. Roessiger.

The Beautiful House in the Eye of the Beholder

by Allan Turner

After teaching for four years in Germany, I didn't come to Switzerland totally unprepared for the European idea of a university. Of course there would be nothing resembling a campus, no student residence facilities, no clubs or societies, no student life as such. On the academic side there would be no tutorial system and precious little in the way of structured courses. In short, there would be no concept amongst either students or staff of the academic community which underlies English university thinking, for better or for worse. And in all this, needless to say, I was quite right.

What I was not prepared for were the side-effects of working in a semi-autonomous department close to, but completely cut off from, the main university lecture and administrative block. I was even less prepared for the stage setting against which my future activities would be played out.

Basle's English Seminar is housed in a 15th century building in the old town, known with very good reason as the *Schönes Haus* ("Beautiful House") and protected by law as a historic monument. It consists of three buildings to be precise, two facing on to the street and one at the back of a small courtyard complete with a large overhanging tree to give shade and a fountain trickling soporifically into its trough. The *Grosser Hörsaal* ("Great Lecture Hall") has a late medieval painted wooden ceiling of which we are immensely proud; so proud, indeed, that we hardly ever use it on the pretext that it is far too large for the size of our classes.

The "Schönes Haus", location of The English Seminar in Basle.
Photo C. Teuwen.

The great showpiece of the building, however, is the cellar. This is ideal to serve as a kind of Elizabethan theater, complete with a gallery and an upper entrance for balcony scenes, and has been used to great advantage both by our drama group and by visiting companies. The only disadvantage is that during the long summer vacation, of course, it's not in use, and for the rest of the year the audience is in considerable danger of freezing to death in the bowels of the earth.

So far so good; almost idyllic you might think. I could almost be back at Cambridge, in a small-scale college without the incessant east wind coming biting across the Fens. But the big difference is that Cambridge colleges were built for educational purposes (whatever Oxford graduates may say), whereas the English Seminar can never escape the fact that it was cobbled together out of three ancient dwelling houses. There is a chronic shortage of usable space which is made all the more irritating by the patent abundance of totally unusable space. Take, for example, the case of the student common room. As it happens, we haven't got one. All the staff of the department have at least a nodding acquaintance with Anglo-Saxon universities and agree that it would be a good thing if a greater feeling of personal involvement could be created within the English Seminar. Accordingly, two or three years ago through the efforts of a particularly committed group of students, one of the unused areas was fitted out with a few second-hand chairs, a table and a coffee machine in an attempt to provide a social focus. A praiseworthy effort, but no amount of commitment could do anything to disguise the fact that this small area has five doors opening off it and practically no direct daylight. The only answer would have been to resite some of the doorways, knock a much larger window in one wall and paint the whole place in bright colours, but unfortunately you can't do things like that with a building that is protected by law as a historical monument! The place remained a cross between a station waiting room and the Black Hole of Calcutta, and the students stayed away in droves until the experiment had to be abandoned. Now the dedicated few prefer an equally unusable but much brighter area two floors above. There they have a cosy corner with easy chairs and magazines, but still hardly anyone uses it. Why not? Because if they talk they disturb the people working in the rooms round about, so they have to sip their coffee in silence, a small academic Trappist community.

Well, even if we can't keep the students in our marvellous me-dieval edifice for long periods at a time, at least we can entice them there regularly by holding our classes in the Seminar, in our own in-timate surroundings, rather than in the central university building with its impersonal rooms and rigid rows of benches, in which the students' eyes are automatically focused on the symbolic lectern at the front and any kind of intercommunication is well nigh impossible. I have never been a great exponent of the cushions-on-the-floor-and-soft-music style of language teaching, but at least on our home ground we can rearrange the tables and chairs to make ourselves feel as comfortable as possible. The problem is that, except for the aforementioned *Grosser Hörsaal* and the reverberating dungeon known familiarly as the Cave, all the possible teaching rooms double up as homes for the various sections of the seminar library.

The seminar library is a marvellous institution. Throughout the whole of my previous career I had been used to a central University Library with vast and awesome arrays of books, together with elaborate electronic security devices to ensure that they were not borrowed illegally. Certainly Basle has a renowned University Library, but the really useful books belong to the seminar libraries of the individual departments. This means that all the books on any aspect of English studies which could possibly interest a student (or, to be frank, most members of staff) are instantly available under one roof - or in our case, as you will remember, under three roofs. Of course, you don't normally have access to German books, French books, books about philosophy, history or economics, because they are all on other people's territory, but what member of the English Seminar could possibly grumble when he has the infinite variety of English literature and linguistics at his fingertips?

The procedure for borrowing books is very simple and very Swiss – you fill in a slip with the title of the book, the name of the borrower and the date, and put it in a small box in alphabetical order. No librarians, no date stamping, no identity cards with magnetic strips. When you return a book, you simply put it back in its place on the shelf and remove your slip from the box. If you want a book that is already out, you look up the borrower in the file and arrange the whole thing with a friendly phone call. Every year at the annual stock-taking we usually discover that about a dozen books have gone AWOL. At this the older members of staff usually shake their heads and make comments about the declining moral fibre of the student body, without stopping to consider that Anglo-Saxon libraries, for all their technological sophistication and eagle-eyed librarians, can lose as many books as this in a week. But then all technical innovation only provides a new stimulus for the human mind, so that most computer fraud, for example, is carried out not primarily for monetary gain but for the challenge which it presents. Why bother to steal books if you can just take them at any time?

Well, actually that isn't quite accurate. You can't take them at any time because, as we have seen, our medieval mansion is

desperately short of user-friendly space, and so library rooms have
to be used as teaching rooms too. So when a dozen or so students are
gathered together for a seminar, the other 95% are effectively barred
from using the facilities. It only needs two seminars to be held at the
same time to have me writhing with frustration because I can't lay
my hands on any of the books I might want. The students take it far
more philosophically: what is the whole of university life if not a kind
of obstacle course to be negotiated?

If this aspect of blocked working space affects all members of the
Seminar, there is one which affects my blood pressure most directly.
The room where I work, or at least where I try to create (for the benefit
of myself and others) the illusion of working, has only one normal
means of access, and that is through the aforementioned Cave. It
regularly happens that I find I need to refer to a book and dash off
towards the library, only to discover that someone is lecturing directly
in my path. I am then faced with the choice of trying to creep out
through the Cave and in again without distracting too many people's
attention – although the greater my efforts to stealth, the more pairs
of eyes seem to follow my progress along the wall, and I may even
be aware of a slight falter in the voice of the lecturer as it reverberates
spectrally off the venerable walls – or else I can stay in my room and
twiddle my thumbs for the next hour or so. It's at moments of decision
like this that I see how my fundamental English sense of class
distinction has already acquired a distinct Continental overlay: if the
lecturer is an assistant, I swallow hard and take the plunge, whereas
if it's a professor I may let discretion be the better part of valour and
prefer twiddling.

To my relief, and largely as a result of my constant grumbling,
the Cave has now been officially declared a through room for me and
anyone wishing to come and see me. However, there are occasions
when I have jobs to do which involve a great deal of coming and
going which could hardly be done surreptitiously. At times such as
this, there is no alternative to the old-established short cut. Still, I
can't help feeling that a day will come when I'm too old and dignified
to go jumping in and out of windows!

The actual room in which I periodically find myself imprisoned
is like all the others in which I've ever worked in that every available
space is littered with a confusion of papers, but there the resemblance
ends. In Germany I had a bright, airy room, modern but just a mite
soulless, with Venetian blinds which came whirring down

automatically in the summer as soon as the temperature reached a certain point. Here I have a beautiful old window with traditional Swiss shutters both inside and out and any amount of soul. I must admit I haven't actually tried shutting the shutters. It wouldn't make any difference anyway; the street outside is so narrow and the house so high that not a single ray of sunlight ever comes to overheat the occupants, not even at noon on Midsummer's Day. When the heating is turned off in the spring, I nearly freeze to death.

However, discomfort and frustration are the occupational hazards of all people who live or work in a medieval building, and it would give a very one-dimensional picture if I were to depict only the spaces (usable or unusable) of the *Schönes Haus* without trying to communicate its atmosphere too. In fact the University of Basle is an almost perfect microcosm of the Swiss Confederation, with its more or less autonomous departments held together by a minimal university administration. The English Seminar, self-contained in its patrician dwelling, represents a small Canton with strong ties of kinship – at least among those students who are not put off completely by the building and its infamous lack of a social focus. For those who have braved the rigours of the spiral staircase in the tower, it is relatively easy to make contact with staff. This contact, taken so much for granted in the Anglo-Saxon educational world, is by no means inevitable in Continental universities, and it is seldom that there is as much closeness as here, conditioned as it is by the nature of the building. Twice a day all the staff, from professors to student assistants, sit down with one another and have coffee, which, in the absence of anything resembling a Senior Common Room, is an ideal framework for the exchange of ideas and information.

This also means, of course, that staff are particularly visible. Although officially I have office hours when students can come and see me with their problems, I usually spend it alone, because everybody knows he can approach me at any time as I wander around the department cursing about its structural defects, and of course that is as it should be.

Needless to say, there is still more that can be done to build up the family atmosphere and offset some of the problems of the buildings. Part of the library lends itself well to the periodic tea parties which seem to have become a part of our tradition, intended to draw new students into the family and give all members a chance to talk to one another. On occasions like this I'm even prepared to forgive the misuse of library rooms. Then it has always grieved me that Christmas always passes without any form of official departmental recognition, so the latest project is a Christmas Evening of Music and Poetry, an attempt to harness some of the considerable talent amongst our students for things other than translations or seminar papers; it's also one of the few things for which the *Grosser Hörsaal* provides an ideal setting.

There is one other traditional Swiss feature which is reflected in the English Seminar, whereby the students can participate directly in the working of the department: the general departmental meeting, normally held once a semester, forgetting a slight hiccup just at present, resembles nothing so much as the traditional assemblies still held in the more conservative parts of Switzerland, where all the male members of the community meet to vote on local issues by holding up their knives. Perhaps something of the medieval surroundings has rubbed off!

A symbol of direct democracy. Photo SNTO.

Hard Rulings on Soft Ice

by Stanley Mason

My eye once caught a small placard hanging in a Zurich tram. It depicted a boy licking an outsize ice-cream (in full colour) and bore the moving lines:

Wir gönnen allen den Genuss,
Doch bitte nicht in Tram und Bus.

Which being translated (supposing you could really translate from one language into another, as people pretend) mean approximately: We wish you joy of your ice-cream, but please don't eat it in tram or bus! In other words – Anglo-Saxons with their generous conceptions of individual freedom will hardly credit it – the city transport authorities were telling their passengers that it was forbidden to eat ice-cream in their conveyances.

This curtailment of personal freedom is quite typical of Germanic – in this case German-Swiss society. There are a lot of things you are not allowed to do, and a lot of people who are prepared to tell you so. I got very angry on my first visit to Zurich before the war when I wanted to jump out of a moving tram – they were open in those days – as we had always done on the buses in Blighty, and a staunch Swiss citizen deliberately stood in my way. I either had to give in to his petty tyranny or to take him on, like Jacob with the angel. Perhaps because he looked very determined – many Swiss do – I gave in, but I seethed inwardly. Later I discovered that you are not allowed to beat carpets or cut the lawn between twelve and two, as it might disturb neighbors who are having a nap. Nor are you supposed, if you live in a flat, to take a bath after ten o'clock at night. The Swiss obviously rank rest above cleanliness, which in my Anglo-Saxon home used to come straight after godliness. And once the house caretaker came to tell me that I wasn't allowed to feed the gulls, for as they flew around the house they sometimes dropped excrement on it. I felt like dropping excrement on him.

How can it be that the Swiss, and the Germans for that matter, meekly accept regimentation of that kind? One of the answers is that they have an innate respect for authority, for what in German is known as the *Obrigkeit*. It seems to have remained with them from feudal times – they have simply never had their social revolution. The

Austrians are regular worshippers of the *Obrigkeit,* especially if it
carried the flag of nobility – Yes, Your Grace, at once, Your
Excellency, kiss the hand, Mrs. Countess. They're on their knees and
willing to serve as soon as they hear a name out of the peerage or one
of their innumerable titles. Without this Germanic readiness to take
orders from those in authority over us, to spring to attention and toe
the line, there might never have been a Nazi episode in European
history. But what of the son of William Tell? After all, did they not
defend their independence in many battles? They did, but this belief
in independence can perhaps best survive in a society that recognizes
a certain *espirit de corps,* so that the individual is ready to accept the
demands and requirements of his society. This sense of belonging to
a community and having to bear a social responsibility is very strong
in the Swiss. The British say "they" when they refer to their
oppressors, and think of some anonymous power above them, the
Establishment perhaps. The Swiss say "we". Each person feels that
he has his place in the social order. There is comparatively little
vandalism in Switzerland, because each Swiss realizes that street
lamps and railway carriages really belong to him and it's up to him
to look after them.

So the Swiss can be told, without a revolution and almost without
a bat of the eyelid, that they are not to eat ice-cream in the tram. One
wonders, anyway, why this should be demanded of them. Simply
because these terrible soft ices have a habit of falling out of their
cornets and making a disgusting mess on the floor? It is a fact that
Zurich station and its environs are strewn in summer with patches of
something indefinable, as though a terrible accident had taken place
here. These are the remnants of soft ices.

I remember that in the buses I used to travel in as a boy in England
there was a notice that said "Spitting strictly prohibited, penalty 5".
I even seem to remember having seen something of that kind more
recently, but the penalty had gone up to 20. Obviously, some people
today might think that 5 is a small price to pay for a good spit. I'm
not quite sure how the thing worked, whether the conductor, if he saw
you spitting, could simply come up to you and say, "I seed yer, mate,
'and over that five quid," or whether you had your name and address
taken and a policeman came round the next day and said, "Missus,
your 'ubby 'as been seen spitting in a public conveyance, that's a
fiver you owes us."

Admittedly, the mess made by a soft ice is much greater than that made by even the most accomplished product of the veteran spitter's art. And ices have become caducous since they went soft. In a way it may be a blessing that they slip away before you can eat them, for their smoothness is usually due to a methyl cellulose product which is also used for making concrete more manageable, and though the manufacturers say it is harmless, we know that it is only after many moons that scientists discover that the things we have been eating for years – spinach, or saccharine, or bacon fat, or even sugar – are really a grave danger to our health. Not that it matters so very much, after all. Each of us can only absorb a limited amount of food in his lifetime, and in this sense every mouthful and every lick brings us nearer to our grave, whether we take it legally in an expensive restaurant or illegally, and in flagrant violation of the decrees of the bigwigs of Zurich public transport, in the form of a soft ice in a tram or bus.

Stanley Mason. Photo R. Bonner.

Letter to a friend in India

by Riz Careem

Dear Ram,
I do wish you had asked me something simpler. Like how it feels to see all those fantastic things in shop-windows here. But you want my impressions on life in Switzerland. On the other hand, the complexity of a Swiss shop-window would warrant an in-depth study of the Swiss psyche itself. Therefore I shall opt for your request.

No, the Swiss definitely don't go to work yodelling all the way in buses and trains. Nor is the entire work-force employed in the manufacture of watches and cowbells. Now they are more interested in the genetic engineering of cuckoos. Also in clocks which forecast the time when Wall Street will have a bear-market. No sir, there is no dilly-dallying here like back at home. Everybody's running against time to the point that if you want to know what time it is, you have to ask "How làte is it please?" Whatever the time, it's already late. That is why everything here is so efficient. Time here does not allow most people to go around yodelling.

Most people keep much to themselves and if you even whistle on the streets you'll get curious glances. I think this is because whistling has no economic purpose in this society. Purpose is written on everybody's face here. Even a drunk has a purpose here. The fact that his brain cells may be partially or, as sometimes happens, fully

Riz Careem and his Swiss-curry restaurant. Photo R. Bonner.

scathed is of no consequence at a Stammtisch**. *The* Stammtisch *in a restaurant is the watering-hole where domesticated animals like husbands come to air their views on anything and everything under the sun. It is very important that you don't let anyone else talk and if per chance someone else does talk, you offer to buy him a drink. The upshot of all this is that everyone starts talking and buying drinks for everyone else and it makes no difference at the end of the evenings if anybody has a clue as to what the topic of conversation was. Everybody retires happily for the night, including the owners whose dream of a holiday in the Adriatic coast is beginning to materialise in the cash register.*

Holidays. This is a phenomenon dear to the Swiss heart and nowhere in the world is it more talked about, written about and sold about as in Switzerland. Planning your holiday starts after the first day at work following your last holidays. No self-respecting Swiss will go where other tourists are to be found. They leaf through brochures full of pictures of palm-lined beaches with no other human being than the native girl in a partial state of undress. Who cares that she was especially flown in for a photo-session from Paris where she is attending a school for fashion-models?

When finally the Swiss family Robinsons arrive at their dream resort, the whole place is swarming with peach-coloured flesh in various shapes and sizes and in varying degrees of over- indulgence. Such a Swiss family is disappointed and crest-fallen for about two hours after which time they meet up with another Swiss family who too have a mutual dislike for other tourists. Then they all spend the entire holiday lamenting the vulgarisation of travel and its corruptive influence on the natives while regularly getting plastered at the bar of their 3-star hotel. I tell you my friend, if you can persuade a financier to put up a 3-star hotel in some remote and drought-stricken region in our country, we can be in business.

Of course not everyone wants a sun-drenched beach holiday. Our town has a bowling club called the 'Kegelverein' and all its members are men. Once every 2 years a holiday is organised for them, usually in a place of exotic culture like Bangkok. I didn't know that bowling is regarded with such passion in Bangkok.

Then there is the weekend. You'd be surprised to know that even in a prosperous country like this, shanties do exist. Yes, real-life

** Stammtisch, a restaurant or pub table reserved for customers who meet there regularly.

shanties with whole families, the difference being that these are occupied only on weekends. They are called 'Schrebergärten' here and like in India, they are usually situated on the periphery of big towns. Unlike those in India they are arranged neatly in rows with a plot of land allocated to each family. These weekend inhabitants are, without exception, apartment-dwellers from the town, some of whom drive up to their humble abodes in Mercedes and BMWs. I used to wonder why they had to undergo such hardship when they could easily afford to buy provisions from the supermarkets, till one day I asked a dweller why he toiled so much. He replied that it made him feel relaxed. If only the peasants in our country would realise what a relaxing occupation they have, they too could be driving Mercedes and BMWs instead of quarrelling with the government over land reforms.

Toiling in a weekend shanty is by no means the only form of relaxing. Relaxing, like holidays, is big business here. It is not done in the way we do back home when grandfather would belch loudly after dinner and go sit under a tree to spin yarns of yore to the rest of the family. Here it means spending a lot of money at the fitness-center to peddle like mad on a stationary bicycle while staring at a blank wall in front of you. Try it and you'll see blank walls in front of you for a whole week.

Swiss-style shanties and a Mercedes. Photo J. Purnell.

In order to relax you have to have an entire paraphernalia of consumer goods ranging from tools, equipment, clothes, sunshades and then some. Take a simple activity like fishing. You and I went fishing with a bamboo rod, a piece of string, a bent pin and a piece of lead. For you and me a reef on the sea to stand on was paradise enough. Here, to start with, you must have the right clothes or uniform. Khaki and muddy-green are the standard colors although now and then you may see an ageing hippie in blue jeans, but he is an outcast amongst the fishing elite.

Before you purchase your angling kit and attire you need a license from the local constabulary who also issues a booklet with all the regulations about where, when and how one must go fishing. You can't just use any bait you like, nor any weight for a sinker. If the license is for a particular lake, the weight of the sinker and the type of bait vary from one part of the lake to another. By the way, the Swiss have no seas as such, so they use the euphemism 'See' when what is meant is lake.

Euphemisms are used commonly here. A Swiss who has been brought up in another country is called an 'Ausland-Schweizer', meaning foreign-Swiss. I have a Swiss friend who was brought up in the States. He tried very hard to shake this label off, but in vain. In his search for an identity he resorted to writing poetry in English instead, and thus he seduced the classier Swiss women. The curious thing is that he too is entrapped in this euphemism-syndrome, like when he invites me to dinner and calls it a feast. In my innocence I never pictured a dish of Chile-con-carné and a nondescript bottle of Chianti as a feast. Maybe it is the language of poets. Maybe the Swiss are a nation of poets.

Another form of relaxing here is hiking, which German speakers call 'Wandern'. Now how about 'wandering' as a euphemism! On sunny weekends everybody goes wandering in this land. If it conjures up images of the Australian aborigine doing his walkabout in the bush or the Swami or Fakir chanting to the rhythm of the tambourine from village to village in India, you are as much in tune with this world as Bing Crosby was with punk music. In this country you wander with an aim and a swatch. As I mentioned before, no one does anything here without a purpose and there is no such thing as aimlessly wandering. Here too, as when fishing, one must have the right attire such as knee-socks, walking-boots, breeches, windcheaters or anoraks and nylon knapsacks, and of course country maps. Some even carry compasses and binoculars. I have even heard it said that one can take courses on wandering, and I tend to believe it since the Swiss are ardent course-goers. The poor fakir in India has no chance against the Adidas-wearing Swiss wanderer.

Most towns in Switzerland are so clean that even if the Almighty himself were to walk along a street and drop a piece of Kleenex on the pavement, he would be reprimanded by the local denizens for ungodly activities. I wish the denizens of Bombay would do likewise. That's the way to attract more tourists and less gods. To the Swiss, cleanliness means tourism as much as godliness. Now they are trying to clean up the stratosphere plus the entire galaxy.

Dear Ram, I am standing in my kitchen admist steaming pots and I can hear the first Swiss clamouring for their curries. I consider my cooking as charitable, as feeding the needy. But now I must stop writing. These Swiss do not like to be kept waiting.

That's all for now.

> *Yours cleanly,*
> *Riz.*

Riz Careem. Photo R. Bonner.

Trying to Tackle It All

by May Zimmerli-Ning

Switzerland was to me a place where the day to day routine did not exist – everyone was permanently on vacation when not selling cheese, chocolate or watches. It was only a matter of time till reality stepped in to demolish this happy illusion.

As a Chinese refugee going to school in England, I had spent many summers in Switzerland visiting the family of a Swiss girl I befriended. Swiss summers in those days were sunny. What a colorful world it was then compared with smoggy London!

Years later, after living a long time in California, I returned to Switzerland with my Swiss husband for more permanent settlement. This time I was armed with our small baby, nappies and the usual ignorance of new motherhood plus a couple of medical degrees and diplomas but without a very clear concept of what was in store for me in my newly adopted country.

Getting started in housekeeping and shopping in Switzerland was, and still is, an experience in public education. I received comments from other grocery shoppers like "Don't squeeze the lettuce!" or "You should come into the store through the 'IN' side." A cashier once told me, "It's not very intelligent to come shopping on such a rainy day with only a paper bag!"

Getting down to job-hunting and working was no less of a learning process. Foreign, married, female physicians in Switzerland must be a rare breed, and those who have children even rarer. To begin with, foreign graduates have to go through their entire residency training again to practice medicine in Switzerland. This requires knowing the local language. I had one of two choices: forget about working, or learn the language in miracle time and go through my medical training all over again. Somehow I had the horrible vision of an emergency station where I would be able to communicate with neither patient nor nurse, let alone prescribe and record medical histories in German, and all this in the middle of the night! No, my courage and perseverance would fail me here, not to think of my family responsibilities on top of it all.

However, I was determined to outwit my predicament and decided to have a go at being a mother and physician. After arranging household help and nannies, I found a half-day job at the hospital experimental laboratory and had then no time left for intensive German lessons. What German I know today is almost entirely picked up by ear and it is predominantly the Swiss dialect. Since there was no actual position at the hospital to fit the job I was given, there were no funds. My enterprising chief got over this snag by allocating the funds available for an absent secretary as my salary. Under the circumstances, maybe I should have considered this an ideal solution, however, I was not satisfied and felt that there must be more fulfilling work for me. Without much analysing, I decided it was a boring job and that I needed a change.

Today I realize that the discontent was because I had no clear concept of what I wished to achieve under the circumstances. Also, I failed then to recognize, or I tried to suppress, the feeling of being an outsider unfamiliar with the medical surroundings, of not knowing the ropes and of being isolated without sufficient knowledge of German. Today I would have done better if I were to start again, but that is another story!

As I said, without much soul searching, I contemplated a change of job. In the meantime we had two more children. Our friends teased, "What awful planning!" They were right. I began to think I might be better off and fulfil my duties better if I stayed home entirely and concentrated on housekeeping and motherhood. I tried this for a year, at the end of which my fourth baby arrived. I was totally inundated and also utterly frustrated by my ill conceived resolution to give up my career. Never mind, forge on!

I applied at a pharmaceutical firm for part-time work and was delighted to be accepted. This provided many challenges for me, my husband and children. I could write a book about the string of domestic help and nannies that have come in and out of our family over the years, about many positive and negative experiences with them. Between each crisis, I overcame the difficulties with the varying school timetables and the constant coming and going of the children by purchasing several alarm clocks with different tones, which were set to go at different times so that the younger two who could not yet tell time would know when they should leave the house to go to kindergarten. I wished I had my family closer at hand to step in during such crises and to be at the receiving end of my torrents of grievances! I missed a support system.

In those days, contrary to Swiss custom, our house was left unlocked to make it easier for the children to come in and go out. All was safe then. Today our children hide the key in a secret spot which

Women in Switzerland who have children and hold down a job are under considerable stress to organise their family's lives so that everything runs smoothly. Photo SNTO.

has since been discovered easily by many tradesmen. For years burglars could have helped themselves! Fortunately no disaster occurred. The only time burglars paid us a visit, to our surprise, was once at night when we were all at home while our garage door was left unlocked.

My eldest daughter said to me one day when she was about twelve, "I would work outside the home too when I grow up, but I would be home when my children come home from school!" I tried to imagine myself running home at four different times during the day, then I put that idea behind me. I did not want to be defeated just because of a school system that required each of my children to be in school at different times each day and to come home for lunch. The school system ought to change, I thought, not me!

Some of my Swiss acquaintances could not understand why I wanted to bother with a job when I have all these children. At my office, they also wondered why I did not stay home, bake cakes and look after my children. My boss said to me: "Part-time workers won't get promoted," and I sense it all too well that women, professional or otherwise, are generally not taken too seriously in the work place. It is not surprising then that a Swiss employer judges job applicants and considers lay-offs partly on the basis of whether there is a family to support. If so, this will be in a man's favor, but the existence of young children works the opposite way for women. Double standards were not invented by the Swiss, but the big difference between the Swiss and others is that they are proud of it. Three cheers for honesty!

Many times I have attended lectures and seminars on feminine issues concerning working conditions or new laws for women. Advancement for married working women with or without children, foreign or otherwise, is very limited. I have been told that most working women have no purpose, direction or aims, that women are less ambitious, less confident of their capabilities and that they do not take matters in their own hands as their male counterparts will do. Surely there is much truth in what has been said about women. This state of affairs is the inevitable consequence of the overall attitudes existing in Swiss society combined with many women's individual character and upbringing.

My personal frustration has been the feeling that I had to adapt all the time and that I could not advance as I had wished. My Swiss husband, being one of the few poor souls with a wife working outside the home, has had to make some big compromises too. To be sure, he did not have to change his job or adjust his hours at work for the same reasons. However, he has had to change his thinking and adapt his role as a partner of a working woman as well as that of a husband and father. For many Swiss men, this is still unacceptable since they are influenced by the fallacy that when a wife works outside the home, this implies her husband cannot earn enough to support his family!

While most men are proud of their sense of responsibility when it is there, my husband, like most of his countrymen, does not even realise that he has it. He is also not aware of any reversed discrimination. It was recently confirmed to me that should I die before him, he would not be able to benefit from my pension. A widower's pension does not exist. The government of this patriarchal society had not reckoned way back then that one day there would be Swiss housewives working alongside or instead of Swiss men.

Foreign women married to Swiss wishing to continue their careers should first have a very clear understanding of the structure of the Swiss society and then make careful plans of attainable goals in the adopted country. The local language should also be mastered. Having a supportive husband is a prerequisite. When these requirements have been met, surprises will not be overwhelming. If I had to do it all over again, I would have taken an intensive psychoanalytical course to discover what I wanted my personal goals to be before I arrived in Switzerland!

Native Foreigners?

by Annette Keller

Believe it or not: being from Zurich and living less than 100 km away in Basle is just as difficult as being a real foreigner in Switzerland. Maybe that's what makes living in this country so hard.

When I first moved to Basle I joined a *Fasnachtsclique***, I tried to speak *Baseldytsch*** instead of *Züritüütsch***and I prepared *Hypokras*** and other Basle specialties. I am so glad that I have left this phase behind me now. But, to tell the truth, from time to time I also feel as if I am a stranger here and I am probably reminded of this just as often as any of the real foreigners here are.

I'm told, "What do you know about this? I have been living here longer than you have." Or, "Well, that might be true or possible in Zurich, but here..." These are just two of the sentences I have to hear all the time. But I probably could not go back to Zurich either because there one would say, "Oh well, you have been away so long – you do not know what it's like here now."

In the States this would not happen. Or would it? I'm not quite sure. Can someone who grew up in the Deep South ever feel at home in the North? How about England? A Scotsman moving to London, somebody from Brighton moving to Manchester? I would like to know whether there are similar feelings there. I do know about Italians from the South moving up North and about those from the North moving to the South. And I do know what Parisians say about any poor Frenchman not coming from Paris. Or what a Czech says about the Slovacs and vice versa. Maybe this is a European problem, but maybe only on the Continent. I really would like to know...

** *Fasnachtsclique*, a 'club' of fife and drum players. They are the heart and soul of the Basle Carnival held at the end of each winter.

** *Baseldytisch*, the Swiss-German dialect spoken in Basle.

** *Züritüütsch*, the Swiss-German dialect spoken in Zurich.

** Hypokras, a special Basle drink served at Christmas and New Year.

Native Foreigners?

by Annette Keller

Although Helvetia symbolizes Switzerland, this monument of her overlooking the Rhine in Basle made by Swiss sculptress Bettina Eichin shows her in a pensive mood. Photo A. Reuter.

Report from the Promised Swissland
by Roger Bonner

Have contracted an irritating skin rash
from too much milk.
Fingers stick to everything –
perhaps the chocolate...

Natives not too friendly; is it gastritis
or shuffling to banks for latest interest
rates, or just depreciation of the soul?

William Tell is doing a brisk business
peddling apples and crossbows.

Per capita income squats like a sandbag
on each doorstep.

The cradle of democracy is rocking on
an alp of neutral snow.

But this is the Promised Land and who am I
to complain – a tick on the haunch
of the Golden Calf.

And then I love so many things: timetables,
the thrill of arriving and departing dead
on time.

I love sunrises and alphorns blaring across
valleys where cows, like great polka-dot
pillows, clang their bells in meadows
lush with tourists.

I love the holes in Swiss cheese,
bread sweet and crusty on pine tables
along with red wines of the Valais
and slabs of smoked bacon.

I love riding in postbuses swerving down
hairpin bends, their triple-tone horns
resounding through chasms veiled by plummeting
waterfalls below forests thinning to peaks
like fists that rap on the sky boomed by
Swiss Air Force jets reconnoitering
the army forever clashing in the hills,
firing canons at an imaginary enemy,
and cracking the window panes in chalets.

And finally I love sleepy train stations overgrown
with geraniums on window sills where plump matrons
lean out waving to postmen.

The footpaths are all signposted and I've been
rambling for years, looking for a way out.

The passes are blocked with boulders of plenty.

The 'Devil's Bridges' of the St. Gotthard pass. Photo SNTO.

A Silly Search for a Perfect Zoo

by Dianne Dicks

"Back home again in Chipiana" sang the circle of chipmunks loudly and gleefully while celebrating Nutsgiving, a very special holiday in North Ambiguous. The big family of chipmunks were dancing around their latest harvest of fresh nuts. Except for Fissy. She was high up over their heads occupied with one of her wild ideas, dashing from limb to limb in a tree-top.

"Come on and dance too, Fissy," one of her sisters yelled up at her.

"Yes, climb down here before you fall, Dear," beckoned her mother.

Her oldest sister squealed loud enough for everyone to hear, "What crazy idea are you up to this time, Fissy? Has that kink in your stripes got the best of you again?" She was referring to Fissy's funny stripes. Most chipmunks have thin white stripes from their noses to the tips of their fluffy tails. Right on top of her head, Fissy's stripes had a funny kink in them. She was always teased about that being the reason she looked at many things differently.

"I wanna get a glimpse of the perfect zoo," she hollered down to the others almost in mid-air between limbs.

Some of the chipmunks stopped dancing and scampered over, squinting to see Fissy up in the tree. "The what?" they asked in unison.

"The perfect zoo," she yelled down to them.

"Can you see it?" asked one of the cousins who promptly got punched in the ribs by another chipmunk.

"No, you dummy, don't you know there's no such thing."

"Fissy says that's where all creatures want to go to find peace, harmony and happiness," explained her mother. "She read about it in a book she found on her favorite moss patch. Now she thinks all civilized animals have to live in zoos and she claims there is a perfect one in Snazzyland, far far away."

Fissy's father joined them and said chuckling, "Don't worry. It's just one of her silly ideas again...that kink in her stripes, you know."

Swaying on the highest twig, Fissy clung to the top branch imagining how it would be to live in Snazzyland and wondering if the residents in the perfect zoo could also speak Wiglish. Her family of chipmunks spoke Wiglish which had become a very special language among animals all over the world. But the Wiglish in Chipiana had a twang to it. Whenever Fissy travelled with her family to other parts of North Ambiguous, she noticed how other Wiglish speakers would snicker about their accent.

When Fissy finally scrambled down to the ground again, her family had already gallivanted off to celebrating somewhere else. Fizzy was proud to be one of those silly, light-hearted creatures that scurried around day in and day out at all sorts of useful as well as purely frivolous activities. She had been president of the Nut-Appreciation Society, an active member of the Chipper Song Association, and elected as cheerleader for Chipiana's renowned basketnut team. She had even won a few prizes for her stories in Wiglish. Eventually all her busy activities paid off in her getting a chiplarship to study chipmunkology.

But of all her activities, Fissy loved nothing better than rolling up on a soft cool patch of fluffy moss to relax and let her imagination fly. There the air smelled delightfully fresh and sweet, the cool moss warmed her heart and the gentle sunlight sparkled in her soul. A good read, rest or snooze in moss seemed to charge up Fissy's inner battery. Afterwards she could whiz happily from one activity to another, sparked with new life and energy.

Shortly after that Nutsgiving party and a beautiful dream on a moss patch, Fissy made up her mind. Later the word spread to all her family and friends that she planned to move to the perfect zoo in Snazzyland. Everyone tried to convince her that she was foolish to leave Chipiana and downright stupid to leave North Ambiguous.

Fissy's dad warned her, "You're too gullible, my dear, and much too naive for such an adventure. You should stay with your own kind!"

Fissy's mom understood her desire to see the world but was also afraid of what would happen to Fissy while living with various wild beasts. She cautioned her, "Go if you must, but whatever you do, watch out for bears."

Even in those days, Fissy had a mind of her own but her adaptability and adventurous spirit had always come to her rescue when her silly ideas took over. In spite of everyone's dismay and foreboding, Fissy set off happily for the perfect zoo which she knew was located in a big river valley in the small mountainous country of Snazzyland.

She'd read a lot about Snazzyland. Its most perfect zoo was known to be immaculately clean, orderly and filled with an amazing variety of most decent creatures. There was a high standard of living there and for generations Snazzyland had been one of the most peaceful places on earth. "Nothing can go wrong there and I'll have a great adventure and learn a lot about the good things in life," she told herself in exhilaration. She knew nothing of any of the languages spoken there. But in a place renowned for its educational standards, she was sure she would find many friends who spoke Wiglish.

As could be expected with her personality and under those circumstances, Fissy was euphoric upon her arrival in Snazzyland. She couldn't stop raving, "Oh, everything's adorably quaint and picturesque, just as I imagined it. Look how tidy, how immaculate. What luxuries! I just can't stop scampering around all the lovely rocks. There are sport facilities and nuts galore!" She scampered around the numerous, though tiny dwellings which were kept spotlessly clean. "There's an abundance of everything here." Convinced she had made the right decision, she kept sighing in joy, "By golly, this is really a very perfect zoo!" Her letters back to Chipiana were full of ecstatic descriptions.

She was soon able to report that there were many different colonies of different animals in the perfect zoo but socially there were two distinct groups. The natives were those animals who had been born in the perfect zoo and the foreigners, like Fissy herself, were those who had come willingly or unwillingly from other countries to live there.

Although Fissy was a foreigner in the perfect zoo, she was a somewhat privileged one. She realized this when she met the Flamingo clan who spent a lot of time dragging their beaks on the ground. They told her, "At least you've come here willingly and from what we hear, the climate and customs here are not that different from what you had in North Ambiguous."

"Yes, yes, yes, of course you're right," Fissy consoled them, noticing their shivering.

Fissy started talking to everyone she met who could speak Wiglish and discovered that the natives of Snazzyland in the perfect zoo were of an honest and earnest disposition and most devoted to their century-long traditions.

The perfect zoo was located in an area of Snazzyland where Botsch was spoken, a unique dialect of Beutsch. Her first real friends, the penguins, Mr. and Mrs. Plais, were natives and explained to her laughing, "Anyone speaking perfect Beutsch is suspicious around here and the only way anybody learns to speak Botsch perfectly is to be born here!"

Mr. Plais tickled her behind her ear with his beak and whispered, "I guess it's too late for you, isn't it, Fissy." He laughed in such a way that Fissy couldn't help laughing with him.

"Yes, yes, yes, you're certainly right about that," she added giggling, and since that was such a useful phrase she got the penguins to teach her how to say it in Botsch.

Fissy was usually in such a state of enthusiasm, reveling in her new impressions, that she didn't notice some of the natives' astonishment at her garrulous chatter and cheerful antics. Most of the natives in the perfect zoo had been schooled in very proper Wiglish. Her unusual but uncomplicated Chipiana-Wiglish was understood by most, but dubious to some. Fissy found herself getting along fine with everyone as long as she kept smiling nicely and saying in Botsch "Yes, yes, yes, of course you're right!"

With the gracious Mr. and Mrs. Plais she spent a lot of time discovering all the pleasures to be found in the perfect zoo. They went on beautiful hikes and experienced some fabulous sunrises and sunsets together. Fissy admired their orderliness and how they could always be fair and follow carefully the many rules that the natives in the perfect zoo had set for themselves over many generations. The Plais penguins belonged to the group of native animals born in the zoo but they had travelled a lot and were happy to share their experiences with her. Like most of the others in the zoo, Fissy always felt at ease with the Plais couple and she told them sincerely, "When I'm with you, I understand why this is considered to be the most perfect zoo anywhere."

Then Fissy became acquainted with her neighbor, Grunch, the strong and bristlelike grizzly bear. Like her penguin friends, Grunch had been born in the zoo and was a native. He could speak a lot of animal languages and seemed to know everything about everything. At first Fissy was not very good at Botsch, the local dialect, and mixed it up a lot with Wiglish and Beutsch. She'd say to him, "Oh Grunch, I admire you for being able to speak 5 animal languages. And your Wiglish is almost flawless." Her letters to her family back in Chipiana were filled with praise about Grunch. "Dad, I bet you're surprised that a grizzly bear tries to be helpful and see, Mom, bears aren't really dangerous!"

Everyone seemed to have a great deal of respect for Grunch because the natives in the zoo would just let him tell them how to do things. But after a while even she began to realize that most of the other animals were simply afraid of arguing with Grunch. Besides, he never listened to anybody but himself. At first it had been helpful to have a friend like Grunch to tell her how to do things as the natives did. Nobody had ever said "Yes, yes, yes, you're certainly right" to him the way she did. He really loved that. It made his fur bristle.

Grunch had made a great effort to explain to Fissy in his firm clear Wiglish and in endless detail just how important some things were. "You mustn't just curl up on your straw thrown about any old way. It has to be stacked, piece by piece, perfectly. First a row lengthways, then a row the other way. You chatter too much. Here you are expected to speak softly, if at all, around others." Time and time again he would admonish her, "It's absolutely necessary that you be extremely efficient in anything you do. And, above all, be punctual at all costs!"

For a long time Fissy took Grunch seriously. She polished her pool every day, lined up her nuts in a perfectly straight row before dining and cleaned up the crumbs carefully afterwards. She labored away brushing the floor around her nest with her tail. In no time at all, it was no longer fluffy and started to get ragged. She'd ask herself, "Will I ever learn to follow all Grunch's instructions well enough to be accepted by the others in the perfect zoo?"

Fissy's days were hardly long enough for her to accomplish all these tasks in the required dignity and with sufficient perfection to suit Grunch. He always found something to complain about. All she could say was, "Yes, yes, yes, of course you're right." Fissy had always enjoyed challenges and did as best she could.

What she began to miss most of all was moss. Grunch had told her, "Moss is a most undesirable plant, quite indecent. It must be painstakingly removed immediately wherever it starts to grow!" When she finally got a moment away from her many chores and talked to friends, Grunch would frown at her and insist, "You're wasting all your time on mindless chatter!"

A lively otter family lived on the other side of her. A small stream trickled through Fissy's yard before flowing into the carefully manicured garden of the otters. The otters were exceedingly busy all day brushing this, polishing that, stacking this, lining up that. Fissy had the feeling that they actually enjoyed all that work, never stopping night or day. They kept their place spotless for the many parties they gave, serving some of the most exquisite specialties available anywhere in the perfect zoo.

They were very nice and playful as otters are but Fissy got tired of hearing 'you ought to' from the otters. It almost sounded like they were saying "You otter be quiet from noon till 2 pm, you otter straighten up your twigs, etc."

When Fissy invited the whole Otter family over for a swim in her part of the stream, they came but said, "Oh, the stream is too dirty on your side!" When she brought out her simply prepared food, Mr. Otter refused to touch it.

Mrs. Otter confided, "We actually came, Mrs. Fissy, to ask you to remove the weeds on your side of the fence."

"Those aren't weeds, they're blackberry bushes. Blackberries are my favorite dessert. Would you care for some? Just a sec, I'll get you a whole bunch. Just spit out a few seeds along the fence and they'll grow at your place in no time at all!"

Appalled at the suggestion, Mrs. Otter gasped, "Certainly not! We believe you ought to get rid of them." Mrs. Otter seemed to know a lot about principles and said, "This is a perfect zoo. Everybody here ought to keep it as perfect as possible."

Fissy felt like saying "You otters could be a lot more happy if you'd be less perfect," but after all, she was a foreigner here and the natives had been "ottering" around a long time. This time when she said, "Yes, yes, yes, you're right" she felt guilty for saying something she didn't mean, but at least that made them stop ottering at her.

Whenever Fissy could get away from her chores, she loved visiting other animals. She'd watch the ponies taking visitors for rides through the perfect zoo. From the monkeys she heard endless humorous tales about the fascinating observations they made of the zoo's visitors. One day some gorillas asked her, "Can you help us write about our observations in Wiglish? Our reports on the behavior of visitors to zoos are to be published in MONKEY TIMES which is circulated to zoos all over the world. Our scientific observations get all botched up because of our Botsch!"

They all laughed and jumped around so excitedly at their own joke that even the visitors at the monkey house began to laugh back at them.

The elephants too had a lot of interesting work. They took young visitors for rides and put on a show every afternoon. Fissy felt rather unqualified to do anything useful for the others. The other residents in the zoo seemed to have many opportunities to express themselves and enjoy life.

"Grunch," she said one day, "I never have time for anything but my chores around my den."

"So what!" was his only reply.

"But other animals here do lots of interesting things outside their dens."

Grunch began to get angry. "Look at the sloppy way you've stacked your nuts! You'll never become efficient."

"But I'm not the slightest bit happier when my nuts are stacked straight. They taste exactly the same whether I stack them properly or pitch them on a pile. Everyone loves Banke the giraffe and you should see what a mess her house is with straw everywhere."

"The others are only putting stupid ideas in your head. They're all incompetent and inefficient," he claimed.

Fissy and Grunch began to have more and more similar discussions. Grunch always felt he was right. "After all, I was born here and I speak 5 animal languages." He loved arguing and debating which Fissy couldn't stand. He never lost his composure nor did he get loud. Grizzly bears don't have to make much of an effort to be taken seriously.

Fissy stopped saying yes to everything and one day she tried to convince him and herself too, "I can get along quite well in the perfect zoo without your advice!"

Grunch just shrugged his shoulders and sent her knowing glances. "You're being unreasonable and hysterical."

Such comments always prompted Fissy to become just that. She would get increasingly upset until her stripes got kinks in them all the way to the end of her tail.

Fortunately, Fissy got more and more involved in translating other animals' reports from Botsch to Wiglish for other zoos. One day the chance came to move to another chipmunk den on the other side of the perfect zoo. It didn't take her long to decide to move away from Grunch and the Otters. Having met many agreeable colleagues in the perfect zoo, she was angry with herself for letting Grunch have such an influence upon her.

Her new den was somewhat over-grown with vines and since no other animal had lived in that den for awhile, there were numerous blackberry bushes and, to Fissy's great joy, also numerous varieties of MOSS! Soft and luscious, in all shades and textures of green. In only a few days, she felt at home in the perfect zoo as she had never felt before. She had a party and invited all her friends. Mr. and Mrs. Plais arranged the food and the monkeys provided the entertainment. There was even a colossal patch of moss robust enough for Tuffy, her closest elephant friend.

In her new den in the perfect zoo she stopped spending her days fidgeting over her nest and lining up her nuts and spent a lot of time with her new neighbors. With the giraffe, Banke, who could be elegant and wise without pressing her opinions, she would sit on a spacious patch of moss and exchange experiences and observations about animalology. Together they started practicing with the show elephants, dropped in on the orangutans and talked hours on end with them about friendships and the various difficulties many creatures had getting along with each other. Sometimes Fissy wondered if it was her strange Wiglish accent in Botsch that kept others from understanding her.

Wiglish had become ever more important in the animal world and some natives of the perfect zoo wanted Fissy to teach them her language. She started giving Wiglish lessons. Most of her students were already very good at Wiglish but were afraid of making mistakes and wouldn't say anything at all. Fissy tried to do exercises that were fun to convince them that it is not necessary to suffer to learn Wiglish. She'd get them playing games with her nuts, relaxing on her moss and although a few of her students might have thought she was a bit too nutty herself, Fissy got them to speaking Wiglish with each other, one way or another.

She wrote home to Chipiana, "Most of my students are turtles. They are such dears! One cannot help but love them. In fact, everyone in the perfect zoo tries to develop the turtles' way of thinking. They have a lot of perseverance, are extremely efficient and nothing can upset them. Since punctuality is such a virtue to them, most have a watch on each leg and a few of the younger and most fashionable turtles love to show off additionally their newest clip watches on their tails and around their shells. You wouldn't believe what I have to go through to get them to talk! Even outside the Wiglish classes they prefer to be quiet. Each enjoys life in his own shell and on his own

time. Sometimes it's a real strain to my kinky stripes just to get them
to stick their necks out. But I know that it's thanks mainly to the
turtles' influence on all the other animals that this perfect zoo has
profited from generations of peace and stability."

Fissy was soon busy as the bees scurrying from one activity to
another. One evening when she was leaving a nut-committee meeting
she found herself skipping along beside a beautiful white polar bear.

She had to run to keep up with his slow ambling gait. She rattled
off in her friendliest Wiglish, "Oh, hi there. I don't think we've met.
Lovely evening, isn't it? You weren't at the nut meeting were you?
Polar bears don't eat nuts, do they? I've never seen you in the perfect
zoo before. You new here? Hey, I'm Fissy, what's your name?"

He smiled in a charmingly shy way but didn't seem to understand
her. Thinking he might also be a foreigner with some unusual
mother-tongue and that maybe he too could speak Botsch, she tried
again. She had become quite proficient in that language, but to make
it easier for him she pointed to herself and said in Botsch, "Me, Fissy,"
and pointing to him, "You?"

His glance showed his relief that she could speak Botsch. They
finally got to talking, his name was Polter. She learned that he was
one of the natives that had been born in the perfect zoo. Polter did
not say much, but his smooth white fur, his laugh lines and deep soft
voice somehow made her tickle all over. She told herself, "He must
be shy about talking to foreigners and careful about making friends."

Polter spoke only in Botsch and said to her cautiously "I've had
some very disappointing experiences with chipmunks."

Fissy suddenly remembered all her troubles with Grunch and
replied outright, "I don't particularly care for bears either!" When
they parted she was quite sure she would never have to speak to that
bear again.

A few evenings later she was sitting on her favorite moss patch,
relaxing by her pool, admiring the shimmering reflection of a sky full
of stars on the water. She felt free as a chipmunk should, dreaming of
peaceful adventures while munching on a luscious pile of nuts plopped
at her side. Suddenly Polter ambled up to her and, without saying a
word, he sat down and gazed first at the sky and then at the water.

Fissy's experience with bears made her think to herself, "He's
gonna soon gripe about how my floor needs sweeping or how my
nest is full of nut shells or that my nuts aren't stacked properly." She
had just finished playing billiards with them and they were scattered

all over the place. "I swear I'll explode if he says anything about moss being a weed!"

Waiting for Polter to say something, she just sat there trying to think up some witty remark in Botsch to make it quite clear she didn't want any more advice from bears. He said something but at first she was occupied with her thoughts, preparing a well-formulated rebuttal. She didn't understand him. She flashed him a threatening "What did you say?" and was quite surprised to see that he wasn't paying any attention to her at all. He was completely absorbed in observing a tiny ant floating on a leaf in her pool. What a sight! A big bear wanting to rescue a little ant!

"I'm afraid I'd smash it if I tried to get it out of the water with my big paw, but you could surely pull the leaf ashore," he said. This she did and the ant exclaimed breathlessly to Polter, "I'm most grateful pal! How in the world does a feller get a chipmunk's attention! I've been out there yelling for help for an hour."

Fissy had been absorbed with her own thinking and hadn't noticed his admonitions. How grateful the ant was to Polter! Fissy tried to offer the ant a nibble of nut crumbs but he hurried off mumbling something about ungrateful foreigners.

Fissy was ashamed and didn't know what to say. Try as she may she felt she would never learn to judge who was her friend and who was her foe. She was ashamed of being such an incapable idiot for misjudging the personalities of many creatures. She was sure Polter would see what a fool she was and laugh at her Botsch accent or at the kink in her stripes. She started lining up her nuts hoping this would distract him from her tears.

Polter seemed not to notice. "You've got an interesting place. It looks cozy...been playing nuts?...you'll have to come over to my place sometime...especially when I get visitors laughing with my splashing...you'd laugh too if you could see me sit and slip as if by accident down my slide and land with a colossal splash in my pool...just think how silly we'd look turning underwater somersaults together!"

In no time at all Fissy found herself laughing at the visions this big polar bear put in her head. She had never realized bears could be funny.

Polter was able to overcome his shyness and they started talking about many interesting things. "I get discouraged sometimes watching those lions and wolves go about their lives blindly, keeping schedules, growling if someone else gets in their way, always out to make a new successful deal." After a while he stopped, looked at Fissy and apologized, "You must think I'm such a fool. Why have I told you all this?"

Fissy sat down close to him and carefully laid her head on his big paw. She looked up into his big sad eyes and told him. "I've needed a friend like you for a long time. I didn't know bears can be soft-hearted and gentle."

Having Polter for a friend somehow gave Fissy a lot of courage. If people rumpled their noses at her moss patches, she'd invite them over to try one out. Very often this made it possible for her to make some new and valuable friendships.

It wasn't always just the natives in the zoo who would cast her odd glances – eventually she realized that the most severe looks were coming from some of the other foreigners living there too. Most newcomers proved to be very stuck in the ways of their homelands, afraid to try out new customs and equally afraid to continue their old ones from home.

Fissy spent many hours with a playful seal who was from Sane Franchiso in North Ambiguous. Fissy introduced her to the amiable Plais penguins thinking they would soon become the best of friends. But Sealy could be impressively dramatic and refused to be seen swimming with the penguins because "it's indecent to swim in feathers!" She had wanted to live in another zoo in a country south of Snazzyland where a certain amount of chaos put spice in everyone's life. She'd say, "I just can't stand the way everyone here tries to think like the turtles, it drives me up the wall! Having everything ridiculously quiet, clean and punctual takes all the surprises out of life."

Fissy tried to help out a bunch of Wiglish-speaking pelicans, a few from Borquaychesterschire (which Fissy was taught to pronounce in two simple syllables "Bor-ster"). Some of them became her dearest friends. Especially Rolican had a big influence on Fissy. Rolican never got discouraged and would rave at the beautiful scenery when the fish she was given were putrid. She'd flip her long wings happily and freely in the heaviest downpour when most of the others, whether native or foreign, would grumble and complain in their dens and nests. Having Rolican as a friend was a great inspiration to Fissy.

Fissy learned she could never tell about a beast from its hide, size nor sounds. For example, intelligent beings everywhere assumed elephants were tough with their thick skin. How surprised Fissy was one day when her friend Tuffy said, "Look how that little bug bite makes me bleed! It's rather embarrassing! A cousin of mine who works in a circus in Snazzyland wrote to me that she'll probably be living here soon too. She got fired from the circus! During a circus perfoãmance she got frightened by the sudden barking of a tiny poodle dog and accidentally trampled a circus visitor."

"Maybe I've let your thick skin fool me too. May I ask you a personal question?"

"Sure, why not!"

Fissy asked her, "What do you do when you feel like a foreigner here?"

"Hard work, Fissy, that's the cure for all ills," she advised.

Feeling a bit homesick one day, Fissy was delighted to learn of the arrival of Flitter, a squirrel from Chipiana! One would think they could have become the best of friends since they had a lot in common. Flitter went around trying to tell everybody how to do things and kept in her jaw-pouches a full supply of the newest grass seeds from Chipiana. "They're guaranteed to be moss-repellent," she raved.

Flitter had a big store of everything and bragged a lot about her influence and knowledge. Fissy learned from her that it was just as wrong to go around saying "No, no, no! You're not right!" as it was to say "Yes, yes, yes, you're certainly right."

The older Fissy got, the more difficult it was to be able to decide what was good about her life in the perfect zoo and what was bad. She'd ponder, "The good things have their bad sides and the bad things have their good sides."

Once, after all that pondering, she said to Polter, "Sometimes I hardly know who I am myself, let alone how to go about judging what is always right and what is always wrong. Lately the Owl's 'Who are you? Who are you?' keeps me awake all night. Maybe that kink's getting the best of me!"

Polter confessed, "Be glad you've got your kink! Oh, what I'd give for just one of your stripes! Can you imagine how boring it is just to be all white? You should be proud of those stripes!"

Fissy had never thought about it that way before. "You know what, Polter! I'd be glad to give you a kinky stripe if I could. But it'd be white!" They laughed a long time about that. Fissy asked him, "What do you do when you feel down?"

"I romp and play in my pool...I can assure you it's most refreshing."

Time went by and a few grey bristles started appearing throughout Fissy's fluffy fur. Even though the perfect zoo had become her home, she realized the natives would always consider her foreign. After a while she began to wonder how much of her was still part of Chipiana and North Ambiguous and how much of her had become a product of Snazzyland.

She no longer went around saying, "Yes, yes, you're right" but she began to drive some of the others crazy with her silly questions.

She asked Tuffy the elephant, "Isn't it sometimes discouraging to be big?"

Tuffy put her trunk in her mouth and thought for a long time. But she couldn't give an answer to that.

Once with the parrots she asked, "Don't you get tired of just saying exactly the same thing that's said to you?"

"Of course not," they all replied in unison. Then one explained, "Haven't you ever noticed how we get the visitors saying dumb things like 'Polly wants a cracker'? Once we get them doing that we have lots of fun teaching them to say, 'I'm a silly bird!'"

Fissy once asked the monkeys, "How can you stand people laughing at you all the time?"

"Laughing is to us what your moss patch is for you. We'd be bored to death if we couldn't clown around."

Polter had the most patience with her and her questions and he often had some very clear answers. After one long discussion about how to tell the good in life from the bad, Fissy sighed and asked, "Is this really the most perfect zoo?"

Polter thought a long time about it and stretched out his long furry neck, laid his head on the ground, looked straight into Fissy's inquisitive eyes and advised her, "Look into your heart and then you'll know."

She jumped up flippantly, "Oh Polter, don't pull that stuff on me! Maybe polar bears have eyes to see their hearts, but chipmunks don't. What's there to see in my heart anyway?"

"Maybe nothing, maybe you're just trying too hard to see it. Why don't you go stretch out on your moss patch by your pool, close your eyes and look into your heart. You'll learn the answer about your perfect zoo and all the other questions you keep asking. That's the only place to look."

Polter watched as Fissy ran off, made a few circles and curled up on the softest spot of the thick dark-green moss, tucked her bushy tail around her head and her nose into the sweetest smelling moss and closed her eyes. After a while Polter assumed she had fallen asleep. Suddenly, Fissy jumped up and scrambled over to him so speedily that even that big polar bear jolted in surprise.

"I saw it, I saw it!" she squealed happily, jumping around.

Polter chuckled as polar bears do and asked, "Did you learn where the perfect zoo is?"

"I sure did, it's where it always was!"

"And where's that?"

"Well, it always seemed to be someplace else. Now I know where it is."

She didn't continue explaining but started to set up nuts to bowl with.

He smiled and asked, "Well, where is it now?"

She cast him a teasing glance and advised, "Go play in your pool and look into your own heart and stop asking me foolish questions!"

"See, I knew you could do it!"

"Yes, yes, yes, of course you're right...sometimes."

* * * *

Fissy never seemed to run out of wild ideas. From that time on she set about getting some of the other Wiglish-speaking creatures she knew who had lived in Snazzyland a long time to write about their experiences. Maybe it was the kink in her stripes that caused her to come up with such silly ideas.

Dianne Dicks. Photo R. Jeck.

List of Authors and Artists

The following is an alphabetical list giving brief information about each author and artist whose work has been included in this book.

Ramón Aguirre

grew up in the American West. He took his B.A. degree in Spanish and German from the University of Colorado and his M.A. in Spanish from the same university. As an undergraduate he studied at Erlangen-Nürnberg University in Germany and as a graduate at the Universidad Central in Venezuela. After receiving his Ph.D. in Romance Languages from the University of Oregon, he taught at the University of Kentucky. Since his visit to Switzerland during his student days, he wanted to live here, and when, in 1980, the opportunity came to be active in the field of education, he came to Zurich where he now works as a teacher and translator.

Jeffrey Barnes

grew up in England's industrial North-West. He quit the dark satanic mills for the dreaming spires of Oxford, where he studied modern languages. He became a translator after a couple of eye-opening years in marketing in London, left England in 1975, came to Switzerland in late 1979 as a translator for one of the big pharmaceutical companies. For four years he worked for the International Committee of the Red Cross and is now a translator at another big pharmaceutical company. He and his American wife live in Basle.

George Blythe

originated from Nottinghamshire but claims he first started to grow up after a postwar period of drifting, taking embryonic diploma courses in journalism at McGill, Montreal, and in German at Vienna University. This was followed by further peregrinations in Spain, Germany and finally Switzerland. After some twenty years of living mostly in the Basle region, he realizes how seriously the consequences of losing one's baggage can be. Editor of a Swiss company's international journal for many years, he also translated publications on psychiatry before compiling a German-English glossary on the subject – nearly becoming a psychiatric case himself in the process.

Roger Bonner

was born in Geneva and emigrated as a small child to Los Angeles, Cal., with his Swiss father and German mother. There he attended grammar and high school. As an alien resident he was subject to being drafted into the Vietnam war. This situation made him decide to return to Switzerland in 1966 at the age of 21. Although it was his 'home country', he knew little about it, its languages nor its natives. In 1972 he received a diploma from the School for Applied Linguistics in Zurich. "Driftwood", his book of poems and translations, won a prize. He lives in Basle with a red-head and works as a free-lance translator and in-company English teacher for a pharmaceutical firm.

Marsha K. Browne

took 13 years after leaving home in Detroit, Michigan, to get to Basle in 1985. She completed her studies in French and English literature at the University of Detroit and the University of Michigan. An 8-month stay in Paris and relocations first to Boston then to the New York area with itinerant Scottish husband and their three sons helped to fill the years. Now settled with her family in the relative quiet of Aesch near Basle, she has been able to return to her first love, drawing, to help maintain her sanity in a (not too!) Swiss household with four men.

Marcel Bucher

was born in 1929 in Lucerne and grew up in Switzerland. Starting his professional career with forwarders and shipping lines, he worked in Genoa, Geneva, Paris and Bremen. He later worked as a manager for Swiss, American, Peruvian, Indian, Pakistani and Italian industrial companies which required worldwide travelling. Since the early seventies he has been working as a translator and journalist in Zurich writing articles on language problems and cultural aspects. Among his diverse projects are his book giving guidelines for translating and another about the Swiss youth revolt of 1980/81.

Riz Careem

was born with World War II in Galle, Sri Lanka. He has never since got over the shock of human folly. He couldn't finish his studies in England but became a successful dishwasher. He now cooks curries in his own restaurant "Schlüssel" in Unterehrendingen, a remote part of the Canton of Aargau, where he lives with his Swiss wife.

Jacob Christ

completed his medical degrees in Zurich and Amsterdam before emigrating as a Swiss to the U.S.A. in 1952 at the age of 26 to study and work in psychiatry, psychoanalysis and community mental health. He served in the U.S. Navy and became a naturalized American citizen in 1958. He held positions in the faculties of Harvard University in Boston and Emory University in Atlanta. In 1979 he was called back to his native Canton Baselland in Switzerland to become head of the ambulatory community mental health facilities. He lives with his American wife in Basle.

Jane Christ

grew up in Philadelphia, graduated from Bryn Mawr College with a bachelor's degree in psychology in 1960 and a master's degree in social service in 1962. Her career as a psychotherapist led her to jobs in social work in Topeka, Minneapolis and Atlanta. By 1973 she and her first husband had 3 children, one of them profoundly retarded. In 1979 she remarried (see notation about Jacob Christ above) and moved to Basle with her new partner and 2 of their children. She does occasional counselling together with her husband and as her main vocation teaches English as a foreign language to adolescent and adult students in Basle.

Dianne Dicks

grew up in Indianapolis, Ind. and attended Rollins College in Winter Park, Fla. She came to Switzerland on The Experiment in International Living in 1961 and, except for a few years living in Finland, Basle has been her home most of the time since then. She was employed many years in Swiss firms (pharmaceuticals, insurance and banking). Besides her work as a free-lance translator, she is an in-company English teacher and active as a journalist. She lives with her two children and her second Swiss husband in Riehen, who tolerate her endless wild ideas and projects to get people to communicate.

Barbara Bruzgo Higelin

was born and raised in a small coal-mining town near Allentown, Penn. A trip to Europe at the age of 18 convinced her that she would like to come back. After a B.S. and M.S. in biochemistry at Ursinus College and Villanova University and 7 years' teaching experience in the suburban Philadelphia school system, she moved to Basle in 1974 for what was to be a 2-year stay. She taught English to adults at one of Basle's private language schools and in 1978 married one of her students. Her husband being French, they live in Hegenheim in the nearby Alsace. She continues to teach English in Basle when she can fit it into her busy schedule of raising their two children, gardening, travelling and writing.

Patricia Highsmith

was born in Forth Worth, Texas, and brought by her parents to New York when she was six. In 1942 she was graduated from Barnard College, Columbia University, after which she had various writing jobs, and mainly worked as text writer for comic books. Her first success, "Strangers on a Train" in 1950 was filmed by Alfred Hitchcock and many other novels and stories have followed to make her today one of the world's most successful writers, best known for her penetrating psychological insight into her characters' minds. She received two Edgar Allan Poe Scrolls, the *Prix de Littérature Policiére* in France, and silver dagger from the Crime Writers Association of Great Britain. She has travelled extensively in Mexico and Europe (Italy, Greece and England). In the late sixties she moved to a suburb of Fountainebleau where she lived until the early eighties when she moved to the south of Switzerland where she still resides and works today.

Lilliam Hurst-Garbutt

was born in Costa Rica to British Honduran father and a Nicaraguan mother. As missionaries, her parents taught her that some rolling stones just have to work harder at picking up moss, as they trundled her to Panama, Barbados and Trinidad. Her family eventually settled down in California where she received her B.A. in French, after having spent some time in France. Although she never intended to reside in one place long, she has been living in Geneva since 1966 where she completed her graduate studies in French, English and Linguistics. She and her Swiss husband have two teenage daughters. She teaches English in the public school system in Geneva and has little time for rags and sewing but enjoys baking breads whenever she can.

Annette Keller

was born and raised in Zurich and is as Swiss as they come, even to the point of being extremely modest about it. After getting her diploma as a translator, she moved to Basle and, by chance, also started teaching English. She married her former linguistics teacher and has since stopped taking languages, schools or the Swiss seriously. She recently took a job in a bookshop so that she could buy books for two-thirds the price but now usually buys three times as many books. The most stable part of her life is her marriage and her affection for their two children.

Harold Mac Farland

Ex-smoker, was born in 1942 in the nick of time into a family of young smokers. His fondest early memories were of his parents blowing smoke-rings into his face and chatting away through the winter evenings of Detroit. The decision of his iron-willed mother to stop smoking herself, and to stop him smoking too, was successful but ultimately led to his emigration to a land of inveterate smokers in 1968 where he lives with his German wife and two adolescent children. He teaches English and computer sciences to adolescents and adults in Basle and spends his free time in ancient smoke-filled rooms reminiscing about the old days in the new country. When his head clears of smoke, he occasionaly comes up with some poetic ideas or does some photography.

Scott MacRae

grew up in the Scottish Highlands. His M.A. in Edinburgh was followed by a course in educational studies and seven years' teaching experience in Germany and Switzerland. He is now working as a free-lance translator after sixteen years in the pharmaceutical industry. He spends his free time reading novels and occasionally confuses life with fiction.

Stanley Mason

was born in the Canadian Rockies, grew up in an English mining village and came to Switzerland as a teacher before World War II. Two books of his poetry, "A Necklace of Words" (1975) and "A Reef of Hours" (1983) have been published. He has written a textbook on "Modern English Structures", and his play "Send Out the Dove" recently won a Living Playright Award in the US. He worked for many years in a Swiss engineering firm, then on the editorial staff of a leading international art and design magazine. Now working from his home in Effretikon, he is a jack-of-all-trades, and proud to have left his stamp on everything from steam boiler manuals and glaciological yearbooks to works on Yoga, Constructivism and what have you. This year his English translation has been published in metric verse of Albrecht von Haller's famous poem written in 1732, *"Die Alpen"*.

Mark Morrison-Reed

grew up in Chicago and came to Switzerland the first time as a 13-year-old in 1962 and stayed until 1965. After attending Beloit College in Wisconsin, he returned to Switzerland in 1971 to teach at the Ecole d'Humanité in Goldern and at a college in Austria before going back to the States to get his M.A. at the University of Chicago. In 1979 he was ordained as a Unitarian Universalist minister. His writings include "Black Pioneers in a White Denomination" (Skinner House, 1980) and recently completed multi-media curriculum focusing on black involvement in Unitarianism. He is currently a homemaker and a parish minister at the First Universalist Church of Rochester, NY, responsibilities he shares with his wife who is also an ordained minister. In 1987 they were in Switzerland again at the Ecole d'Humanité on sabbatical with their two children.

John O'Brien

born and raised in Indianapolis, Ind., was transplanted to Salem, Ore., at age 11. After college and theology studies in the Northwest, he went to the University of Louvain, Belgium, to study philosophy and went back to the States five years later with a degree, a Swiss wife and a baby daughter. Three years after that he returned to Europe with his family, this time for good. He has been a translator at a Basle dyes and chemicals manufacturer since 1973. Despite certain problems (see article), he manages to get along with the Swiss not too badly; he became a citizen of the country in 1981. He reads avidly, sings in two choirs, enjoys hiking and his occasionally subject to a powerful urge to get out of town and see wide-open spaces. Alas, the urge often comes over him as he sits at his computer in the office.

Anton Rudolf (Tony) Obrist

was born in London in 1927 of Swiss parents. After attending primary and secondary schools in London and Hertfordshire, he graduated in chemistry from the Royal College of Science and did National Service in the British Army for two years before continuing his research and receiving a Ph.D. from London University with a thesis on the thymus gland in neuromuscular transmission. His own neuromuscular efforts in 1954 resulted in his joining a Swiss pharmaceutical firm in Basle as a promotional and technical English translator, which is what, with modifications, he is still doing. He is most interested in the interface between Britain and Switzerland and besides his hobbies of singing and writing, he has been an enthusiastic performer in a local English theatrical group. He and his Swiss wife live in Riehen.

John Purnell

grew up in Welwyn (pronounced 'wellin') Garden City, Hertfordshire (pronounced by most of the locals as 'Arfersher'), and studied in Exeter and London. Having married a Swiss citizen and not wishing to work on Maggie's farm, he came with his wife to Switzerland in 1980 to take up employment as a translator, first at a bank in Zurich and later at a Basle pharmaceutical company.

Kathy Tschurtschenthaler

was born and raised in Michigan and attended Hillsdale College there before studying at the Institute of European Studies in Vienna where she met her husband. They spent a number of years residing in such diverse places as Rochester, NY, Lausanne, Heidelberg and Hong Kong before finally settling down in the Swiss Canton of Baselland in 1966 with their 4 children. Besides teaching English, she enjoys playing tennis, learning French, gardening and participating in a Bible study group. Since one daughter now lives in Greece and another in Texas, her visits with them allow her to keep enjoying the many challenges of cross-cultural relationships.

Allan Turner

was born in Peterborough in eastern England. He is a jack-of-all-trades and a Master of Philosophy in both medieval studies and modern linguistics. Finding his talents unappreciated in his native country, in 1980 he abandoned teaching German to unwilling English schoolboys for the sake of teaching English to marginally more willing German university students. Since 1985 he has co-ordinated the English language courses at the University of Basle. He enjoys wine and music, although not necessarily in that order.

Trevor Watts

originates from Nottinghamshire and, after graduating at Nottingham University, did a PhD at Imperial College, London. In 1968 he accepted an offer for a job from a scientific instrument manufacturing company in north-eastern Switzerland and has been living and working there ever since. He earns his daily bread by organising microscopy courses, teaching microscopy, and doing technical and scientific translations. Trevor Watts lives with his English wife, two children, two cats and two guinea-pigs in the village of Widnau.

Heidrun West

was born in Sudetenland (now Czechoslovakia) and lived in southern Germany until she was 11. Her six years of schooling in Switzerland, in Trogen/AR were followed by studies in Edinburgh and a job in Geneva where she and her British husband married. His job took them back and forth between Switzerland, England and the USA. She received her B.A. degree from the State University of New York before returning to Switzerland in 1983. She has two sons – one an American (because he was born there), the other British (because he was born in Zurich where only his father's nationality counts). Heidrun West no longer knows what her own nationality is, her passport at least declares her as British. She usually feels at home where she can plant a garden. She teaches English and is active as a writer and poet.

Homer D. Wheaton

was born in 1905 in New York City of an old American family with roots in eastern Dutchess County. From 1926 to 1942 he worked in Wall Street, thereafter spending 3 1/2 years in the U.S. Air Force. Returning to the financial district in 1946, he and a friend formed their own investment advisory firm. Since 1955 Switzerland has been his main home. His wife is Swiss. Encouraged and helped by his deceased brothers, both accomplished pianists and organists, he has composed a number of songs, Christmas carols for adults and children, and hymns.

Cornelia Ziegler

was born in South Croydon of German parents who came as refugees to England during World War II. After finishing her schooling in England, she received a scholarship to study at Munich's Art Academy in 1962. She worked there a few years on animated films and at an advertising agency before coming to Berne, first as a graphic designer and illustrator. She moved to Basle in 1972 to work in film production. Since 1978 she has been working free-lance. Her calendars, sketches, portraits and townscapes have been admired at a number of exhibitions. She enjoys putting movement into still figures, sound into colours and life into objects.

May Zimmerli-Ning

was born in Beijing, China. When she was 12, as the communist government came to power, her family fled from their native country and went to Hong Kong. From there the family emigrated to the U.S. She was sent to school in England, returning to her family only after completing her basic studies. She obtained her medical degree from the University of London and did post-graduate studies in the U.S. with specialty training in gastroenterology and liver diseases. She has since gained experience as a physician on both sides of the Atlantic. She met her Swiss husband in New York and they settled in Switzerland in 1968. Her work at a pharmaceutical firm in Basle, her four teenage children and an active social life all leave little time for her to ponder about having had to adapt to different cultures several times in her life.

Teachers' Tips

Classroom Activities with
Ticking Along with the Swiss

by Dianne Dicks

Here are simple approaches for using stories for language learning. These can be used by both teachers with classes and by individuals in self-access.

* * * *

"Tic-Tac"

Before your class reads the story, have your students list some 'virtues' we all strive for, like being

> punctual
> dependable
> hard-working
> determined, etc.

After your students have prepared their lists, in groups of 2 to 3 they compare their lists, adding or deleting 'virtues'. Finally they should number their 'virtues' according to priority.

After students have read "Tic-Tac", either in class or as homework, get the same groups to re-evaluate their lists of 'virtues', discuss any changes of priorities.

Get students to describe the "Frau Hubers" in their town, her appearance and her activities.

* * * *

"Winter in the Ticino"

Before your students read the story, find out how much they already know about Patricia Highsmith and get them to make guesses with questions like

> Who is Patricia Highsmith?
> What kind of stories does she write?

How many books has she written? (more than 27)
Tell your class that Mrs. Highsmith lives in Switzerland and ask your students to make guesses about how a world-famous best-seller author lives:

What does her house look like? (Draw a rough sketch of house on hill according to students descriptions)
Does she have lots of parties? (Class votes yes or no.)
What is her relationship with her neighbors?

After students have read the story, they should compare the sketch made of her houses before with the descriptions in the story and make corrections, perhaps practicing the use of 'do' for emphasis like:

She does live on a hill, but not on top.
She does have parties, but simple ones, etc.

* * * *

"Sisterhood - does it grow in every climate"
or
"On Being on Outsider"

Before your class reads the story, have your students match the following words a) to h) with their most suitable meanings 1) to 8) and mark if the word applies to men, women or both:

a) brotherhood

1) a group of female students at a college or university

b) fellowship

2) a small but 'exclusive' group united by some interest or purpose

c) sisterhood

3) a group 'devoted' to a person, practice or idea

d) clique

4) a group of equals or friends

e) cult

5) the feeling of belonging to a group of women with common interests

f) fraternity

6) a group helping its members promote a particular trade

g) guild

7) a group of male students at a college or university

h) sorority

8) the feeling of belonging to a group of men with common interests

After your class has read the story, have them discuss in pairs a 'group' they belong to and how easy it is for an 'outsider' to become a member. Encourage them to discuss the advantages and disadvantages that such groupings have if they make membership easy or difficult.

****

"A Taste of Home"

Have your students close their eyes and imagine they are living in some other country and that they are very happy there. After a few minutes elicit some examples of the students' dream-countries and what things are available there that they don't have at home.

Once your students have visualized their dream country long enough, explain that now 20 years have gone by since they have been away from home. A friend is travelling to their home country and wants to bring back something from 'home'. Have students make a shopping list of the things they think they would long for from home after being away many years, particularly food items. In pairs, students compare lists.

After reading story, students compare objects mentioned in story with their lists. You list on blackboard the 'souvenirs' from home your students cherish most, then discuss how these items would sell at the students' home-town market place. How does this list compare with the real souvenirs sold in your students' country.

* * * *

"Watch those Wicked Words"

Before your students read the story, present to them a brief list of 'false friends' – words that look alike but have different meaning when used in another language. (For example, 'reform house', 'car' and 'also' in English and German).

After students have read "Watch Those Wicked Words", in pairs they should think up situations where such words could cause funny situations. Have them write up dialogues for these situations and afterwards read and act them out.

* * * *

"In the Swiss Army"

Before the students have looked at the story and pictures, ask them to describe what they think a Swiss soldier looks like. Draw rough sketch on blackboard according to their descriptions and present a simple vocabulary of words used with 'uniforms'.

Then explain that the story is about a Swiss boy who went to America as a small child and who only came to Switzerland at the age of 21 when he had to go into the Swiss army. Students then discuss what they think this 'Americanized' soldier looks like and compare him with the first sketch. Encourage your students to describe the usual 'Rambo' figures they see on TV and in films. Finally get class to vote on what object a Swiss soldier is most likely to have in his hands when being photographed – a rifle, a Swiss Army knife or something else.

Look at first picture of Roger Bonner in the story. How does he compare with the sketches students made? (In the photo, this soldier is holding a broom, has torn, dirty trousers and looks like he couldn't scare a flea.)

After students have read the story, in pairs they prepare a list of features a good soldier should have when **not** fighting.

* * * *

"Unforgettable Experiences"

Looking at the picture of the sign post in the story, students should try in pairs to pronounce the names of the places
Geilisguet, Ramsei, Lützelflüh, Zollbrück,
Ober Rotenbüel, Fluehüsli, Ober Rafrüti, etc.

If you teach in Switzerland, such words will, of course, not be a problem. Select names of places in other countries which are difficult for your students to pronounce, e.g. like Gloucester (pronounced glos-ter) and Oswaldtwistle in England, like Saskatchewan or Chilliwack in Canada, like Chattahoochee, Weohyakapka or Okeechobee in the USA.

Aterwards ask individual students to call out the names of these places as quickly and loudly as possible. Have class choose which places are most difficult to pronounce, which sounds are not in their mother-tongue. Elicit how students feel when they make these unusual sounds, are they shy, embarrassed, insecure, feeling like a clown or silly?

Ask them to make list of words in their languages that they know are difficult for people of other languages to pronounce.

After your students have read the story, ask them how they think it 'feels' to have an accent. Encourage them to discuss their impressions of people they know who have an accent and how much it affects your students' abilities to become friends with these people. Then imagine how these same people would change if they were able to get rid of their accents. How would it change their personalities, their friendships, for the better or for the worse? Should people with accents have 'speech therapy'?

* * * *

"Culture Shock"

Looking at the picture of a cow being transported by helicopter, students list in groups of 2 to 3:

What's new and different for a cow in the sky?

Your students will surely come up with many nonsense statements, if not, provoke them by suggesting

She gets a new view.

She can take the weight off her feet.

She has an adventure to moo about, etc.

How does a 'cow in the sky' compare with living in a 'foreign' country?

— new sights, sounds, inability to communicate or control situations, etc.

After students have read the story, talk about the things one can do to make friends in a new neighborhood or debate about the pros and cons of the advice 'stay with your own kind!' versus 'force yourself to mingle with the new culture on your own!'

* * * *

"Trying to Tackle it all"

Before reading story, students list typical daily chores of a working man and a working woman.

* * * *

"Native Foreigners"

Ask your students to discuss in groups when they feel like a 'foreigner' in their own country. This is not meant in reference to patriotism for a country but how attached they are to their way-of-life. They should imagine themselves in another part of their own country – city people in the country or vice versa, living with people with another local accent, etc.

After reading the story, class discusses or writes about:

How far from home do you have to go to feel like a 'foreigner' in your students' country?

* * * *

"A Silly Search for a Perfect Zoo"

Before your students read the story, ask them to describe what they think these places or people are like:

a perfect zoo
a place named Snazzyland
a place called North Ambiguous.

Pass out cards and ask each student to write the name of his or her favorite animal on it and give it a name. Collect and keep these cards to use in a lesson after students have read the story.

Explain that many symbols are used in this story. The meaning of words can often not be found in dictionaries because the words refer to something symbolized. Elicit the names students are aware of in their mother-tongue that lovers use for each other (Ducky, Doggie, Pussycat, Bear, Lambkins, etc. have their equivalents in most languages).

After your students have read the story, have them discuss in groups what the following characters in the story would be like if they were real people, things and places:

Grunch
The flamingoes
The otter family
The penguins
The turtles
The parrots
The monkeys
The Nut Appreciation Society
Basketnut team

Wiglish, Beutsch and Botsch
Moss

After they get the feel of these metaphors, pass out the animal cards they made and ask students to be their favorite animal. Instead of being a classroom, you are all in a zoo together. As teacher you are the zoo director and with the help of the class, decide which animals could share lodgings – they then work together in these pairs or small groups. The animals are to agree upon the following:

– at what time will meals be served
– when is 'quiet time' to be observed
– who does the cleaning up
– what function in the zoo they could take over that would help some other animal.

Afterwards the groups report to the zoo director their decisions.

AN INVITATION

to all Readers
Ticking Along with the Swiss

Do you have a story in English about your experiences in living or working with the Swiss?

Maybe it can be included in the next volume of TICKING ALONG WITH THE SWISS.

CONTACT THE EDITOR
IN SWITZERLAND:

Dianne Dicks
c/o GS-Verlag Basel
Petersgraben 29
CH-4003 Basel